DAVID W. SCHILL

"A Case of Mistaken Identity"
(see pg. 83)

To my friends and neighbors in Moorestown. War is not the answer.

David W. Sohill

Before The Memories Fade

An Anthology of
Humorous, Bizarre and Poignant Stories
from The Vietnam Era

by

Lt. Col. Robert W. Michel, US Army, Retired

authorHOUSE™

1663 LIBERTY DRIVE, SUITE 200
BLOOMINGTON, INDIANA 47403
(800) 839-8640
WWW.AUTHORHOUSE.COM

First published by AuthorHouse 10/06/04

ISBN: 1-4184-9943-9 (sc)
ISBN: 1-4184-9944-7 (dj)

Library of Congress Control Number: 2004097039

Printed in the United States of America
Bloomington, Indiana

This book is printed on acid-free paper.

For those that were chosen
All that remains are the
Memories and the names
Carved in stone

Without names, memories are lost
Without memories, the past is lost
And without the past to remind us,
The future is lost.

Les Dawson
LT. Col. U.S. Army Retired

TABLE OF CONTENTS

INTRODUCTION
By Ben F. Rogers III

Lieutenant Colonel, Robert W. Michel, the man who compiled and organized this book, was my friend for twenty-five years. I first met Bob when he and I were dating two women that were best friends. Bob and I double-dated fairly often and found, over time, that the two of us actually had more in common with each other than we had with the women we were dating. We all had lots of fun, they were very interesting and lovely women, but Bob's and my friendship continued long after the double-dating had stopped.

In 1980 we each got the boating bug at the same time and purchased our crafts with the object of living aboard. The location for this flotilla was the Potomac River just south of Washington, D.C. in Alexandria, Virginia, where we had both lived for years. Several other friends of ours owned a piece of the coastline along the river and had allowed us to build a pier for our purposes, and their benefit. We lived along side each other for years and our friendship continued to deepen.

Bob and I eventually each married again and moved away. I didn't get to see him as often as I would have liked for many years, but we were always in touch with each other's spirit through friends and family. When we did see each other, we always had a great time and often spoke of the possibilities of this book. Years before, Bob had told me the story of his encounter with 'Rainbow Charlie' which is printed here along with the memories of the other twenty authors. We discussed at great length the war, our Army years, and the need to give soldiers of the Vietnam era a forum for telling their experiences.

More years have passed since those conversations and many obstacles have been traversed in order for this book to actually be completed. In the early 80's no one was talking about his or her experiences with the war, and if this collection had been published at that time, it would likely have been a much larger economic success. Bob would have liked that, but it wasn't ever really his primary concern or motive. His main objective, as he explained to me many times, often in the wee hours of the morning, was to create an opportunity for others to tell their tales. Even at this late date, that has been accomplished.

My friend Bob died in March of 2004. I asked his wife, Patti, if the book had ever been finished and she told me that it was almost completed and published in 1997. She went on to say that Bob had been diagnosed with lung cancer not long after and, as a result, he hadn't had the strength and stamina to complete his quest. Since then, the book had been stored in a box in the garage until Patti discovered it during a recent move. I asked if I could finish it for him and, thank God, she allowed me to do it.

Soldiers have, for centuries, traveled great distances to fulfill the wishes of their fallen comrades, and the completion of this book has been just such a journey for me. I felt a tremendous responsibility to Bob to complete it, but along the way, I began to feel the same level of responsibility to all the other authors and Vietnam Veterans everywhere. I have tried to include as many stories as Bob had selected and they are printed here in almost exactly their original state. I didn't edit the content, but I did change a word here and there where I felt it was absolutely necessary. Essentially, I edited an occasional spelling, typing, or grammatical error, but otherwise, the author's works are printed as they were originally entrusted to me. The acknowledgements are also included just as Bob had drafted them on his yellow legal pad. The names of some of those acknowledged are not familiar to me, but I was very flattered to find my name among them.

I have never met any of the men who wrote this book, but I feel as though I know many of them better today than I would have, if I'd actually met them in their daily lives. Their words taught me so much about them, that I think I actually might recognize some of them in a crowd. It was an honor to do this work for Bob, his family, and these men. Like Bob, they are all my heroes. I hope the readers of this book enjoy the experience of these stories and are moved by the spirit of the men who wrote them.

ABOUT THE EDITOR: Benjamin F. Rogers III, served in the U.S. Army as an SP5 Personnel Specialist from May 1971 to May 1975 and was assigned to work with Congressional and White House correspondence as it related to Army Enlisted Men and their families. His responsibilities covered servicemen wherever they were stationed, including all of South East Asia. Ben lives, plays golf, and writes stuff, in San Diego, California with his wife, Margi.

NEVER JUDGE A BOOK BY ITS COVER
By Colonel Gordon A. Larson, U.S.A.F. Retired

It was in the spring of 1967 when I was shot down and captured just outside of Hanoi. I was severely injured in the bailout but that did not stop my captors from subjecting me to sever interrogation and solitary confinement in the infamous "Hanoi Hilton."

In the fall of 1967, I was moved to a smaller camp in Hanoi and put in a cell with two other POWs. One of them was also injured; the other was there to help take care of us. Talking out loud was forbidden, and we were prohibited from seeing any other prisoners. We were never allowed out of our cells when any other POWs were out of theirs. The cell had no windows and the walls were of foot-thick cement and bricks, intended to keep us from communicating with any others in the camp. The punishment when we were caught was usually very severe. However, communication with other POWs was very important to us for peace of mind, and we devised many ingenious methods of doing so. Primary was the "Tap Code" which consisted of tapping on the wall in Morse code, sweeping a series of brush strokes with a broom, or putting notes at drop points in common areas of the camp that were written in "Tap Code".

One day I was at the wall 'tapping' with Lieutenant Colonel Herve Stockman, the Senior Officer in the camp at the time, when he informed me that for a little diversion, he was going to initiate a contest whereby the winners would receive a bottle of Brandy or Cognac from him upon our release. There would be a prize for the crewmember that bailed out from the highest altitude, the lowest altitude, the fastest speed, and the slowest speed. I felt confident that I would win the fastest speed (Mach 1.15) and that I had a pretty good chance at the lowest altitude (400 feet). Due to the distances involved within the prison complex and the danger of being caught communicating, it took two to three weeks to send a simple message throughout the camp and receive a response.

Weeks later Herve called me to the wall and tapped that I had won the fastest bailout but not the lowest. He asked me if I would believe 30 knots and 20 feet!!! I immediately thought of a helicopter crewman that might have been shot down, and that is the moment I first heard of Apprentice Seaman Douglas Hegdahl. It seems that Seaman Hegdahl was just out of "Boot Camp" and serving on the Navy Cruiser U.S.S. Canberra in the Gulf of Tonken patrolling and firing its big guns at shore installations in North Vietnam. It had been a hot night and although it was against standing orders for crewmen to be topside during engagements at night, Seaman Hegdahl wanted to watch the big guns fire. Just as he got on deck, the ship's guns fired a salvo and Hegdahl was knocked to the deck and fell overboard. Fortunately, the ship was turning at the time, and the propellers did not hit him. As it was night and noisy from the guns firing, no one saw him go overboard or heard the splash. He was without any flotation gear of any kind, and had to tread water for about 5 hours before a North Vietnamese fishing boat spotted him and pulled him out of the water, totally exhausted. To say he was lucky would be an understatement. When he failed to report for duty, an exhaustive search of the vessel was made, and four days later, the ship held a memorial service in his memory.

It was not until many years later, after my release from prison (1973), that I heard the "rest of the story". When Seaman Hegdahl was first brought to Hanoi and told his bizarre tale, the North Vietnamese did not believe him and were sure they had captured a "Yankee Spy". All of the other POWs were crewmembers of aircraft that were shot down over North Vietnam. They were in a 24 to 42 year age group and were all college educated. Hegdahl, an 18 year old, with a high school education, was thrust into this setting and unable to see because he had lost his glasses when he fell overboard. He was interrogated for over a month until the Vietnamese were finally convinced that he really was what he claimed to be and that as a low ranking sailor he certainly did not have any valuable military information to share with them.

Hegdahl realized that if he played dumb, he would be left alone. He professed to be unable to spell anything but three or four letter

2

words and could not understand words over five letters. They soon ignored him and let him out of his cell periodically to sweep and do other menial tasks. He was given a roommate on four different occasions for three to four month's duration. It was during these times that he learned of the torture of other crewmembers, the complete lack of medical attention, forced propaganda from the prisoners, but most important, he obtained a comprehensive list of approximately 260 names of crewmembers who were captured and held in Hanoi. On this list, only about 90 to 100 had been declared as captured by the North Vietnamese. The families and our Government did not know if others who were shot down were alive or dead. What the Vietnamese did not know was the Seaman Hegdahl had a photographic memory and could easily remember 260 names, branch of service, etc. It was said that he could and did recite the Gettysburg Address forward and backward!

For propaganda reasons, Seaman Hegdahl was offered release with two other POWs, but refused because he knew that the Senior Officer's desire was that when the time came to leave, we would go home in the order in which we were captured. When it was learned that Hegdahl might be offered release a second time, the Senior Officer in the camp felt that the information he possessed was vital and he ordered him to accept the offer.

Upon his release, Hegdahl revealed not only the aforementioned statistics, but also the exact street location of several of the camps. The Vietnamese were furious and embarrassed by having been taken in by this lowly individual. That was the last time there were any early releases offered by the North Vietnamese.

About a year after my release, Colonel Stockman visited my wife and me in San Antonio. When I opened the door, he stood there grinning and handed me my bottle of Remy Martin cognac that I had won in the contest. He said that he had already awarded Hegdahl his TWO bottles. We spent the rest of the night, and much of the bottle, reminiscing about Seaman Hegdahl and how he had duped his captors-at which time Herve informed me that Hegdahl had been discharged from the Navy, but was now working for the Navy as a civilian escape and evasion instructor.

ABOUT THE AUTHOR: Gordon Larson was Squadron Commander of an F-105 squadron flying out of Korat Thailand, from November 1966 to May 1967, when he was shot down over North Vietnam. He resides in San Antonio, Texas with his wife Mary.

THE CHAPLAIN
By James F. Breen

It is certainly a "Special" Ministry to be a Chaplain in the Armed Forces of the U.S.A., but not as easy as it would seem.

As a young, eighteen-year old grunt in the 1ST Air Cavalry Division, my first exposure to a Chaplain was dramatic, to say the least, but a welcome sight to my sore, lonely eyes. All of them, whether Catholic, Protestant or Jewish, exuded courage. Deep into "Operation Thayer" on the coast of Bong Son, I witnessed such an example.

In flies this Minister in a Huey helicopter sitting next to, and on top of an indiscernible pile of "whatever." He started the service by reading scripture, and when his sermon time as due, you could see he was hesitating. Then with the most honest statement that was unforgettable, he said, "Boys, I came here to preach to you about forgiveness, the peace of our Lord and Savior Jesus Christ, and to love your enemy! But," he continued, "today, I cannot bring myself to do it, and I beg your forgiveness. I just rode in on top of the body bags of six of our brother Sky Troopers who fell to booby traps, small arms fire, and other various and sundry atrocities perpetrated by soldiers of the Peoples Army of North Vietnam (NVA). Four of who by the way, sat opposite me, quite alive, in the same chopper. So boys, my job dictates that I should tell you about all the Christian love that I felt for these captives I rode with on the way to preach to you. And fellows I had a knock out sermon! But I just don't feel like being a plastic, phony S.O.B. In truth, I wanted to kick those NVA bastards out of that Huey so damn bad, it wasn't funny."

We sat in numbed silence! The majority of the men in the platoon were Christians. I was Roman Catholic, so I whispered to my assistant gunner, Saul E. Atkins from Jacksonville, Alabama, "Are most of your preachers this blunt?" He answered, "He's upset!"

James West, a strong Southern Baptist was the first to start clapping and cheering. The rest of us chimed in and rose to our feet, unorthodox to say the least. There we were on top of this high mountain with the enemy all around us, and we were whooping and hollering and smacking the Preacher on his back with gusto.

PFC. Lorenzo Grayson, a very clean cut, prayerful African American from Prichard, Alabama, and the son of a Baptist minister, lifted his M-16 rifle high in the air and yelled above the hilltop winds, "My brothers, we all have one prayer that we know! Let's join with the good Reverend Allen here in prayerful thanksgiving for the gifts he brought us on this windy mountain."

"Our Father, who art in Heaven…."

It must have looked wild to any spectators in the area. A platoon of filthy, tired, Sky Troopers alongside a Chaplain wearing "Camouflage" vestments praying the Lord's Prayer. But it felt good!

Thank you Chaplain Allen! … Wherever you are!

ABOUT THE AUTHOR: Jim Been was a Machine Gunner in "D" Company, 2nd Battalion, 12th Cavalry Regiment, 1st Air Cavalry Division, from May 1966 until he was wounded in February 1967. He resides in Newtown, Pennsylvania with his wife Helene.

CALAMITY AT 2000 FEET

By William Slusher

One might expect that the first helicopter aerial dogfight in the annals of aviation would be fought during Desert Storm by one of the exotic new rotary-wing gun ships like the AH-64 Apache, or at least a Cobra. But it wasn't. No one could have expected that there would be a lot more than just helicopters that went into this historic event, so let's just start at the beginning.

In 1967, a high school junior could be given the aptitude testing and physicals for the Army helicopter pilot course, and if he qualified, he could be offered a guarantee of flight school after basic training. No college degree was required. All that the accepted candidate needed to do was graduate high school and be eighteen years old by the time he entered the Army. Consequently, it was possible that a kid could do eight weeks in basic infantry training, nine months in helicopter flight school earning his wings, and ship right out to Vietnam. He could then fly co-pilot for a few weeks, and wind up a combat aircraft commander with his own four-man crew and helicopter while he was still a teenager. The upside of this phenomenon was that you had a hell of a lot of young, hotshot aviators with bulletproof self-images who did things with helicopters, including thousands of miraculous rescues under fire that experts said couldn't be done. The downside was that you had your occasional shortfall in good judgment. This is where I come in.

I was an "old man" of twenty-two and a combat veteran pilot of over a thousand flight hours when I approached my ragged, dirty, over-worked old Huey on the day of the first helicopter aerial dogfight in the history of the world. I wore wrap-around sunglasses, a two-piece Nomex flight suit, a Ruger .44 Magnum in a gunslinger holster, and a tail-rotor pitch-chain bracelet on my wrist. I was unquestionably the coolest thing that ever strode the planet Earth.

7

I went over the logbook and the aircraft with Moses, the black crew chief whose courage and mechanical skills were many times the salvation of my crew. The gunner, buck-sergeant Reuter (long since bastardized to "Roto-rooter") was securing well oiled, M-60 machine-guns to gun bay swivel-posts at the aft sides of the cargo floor. My co-pilot for the day, Warrant Officer Mike Gavich, entered the revetment, shortly after having attended a briefing at flight operations to obtain our initial mission for the day. "Major says haul ass over to Division Re-supply and take some hot load they got out to LZ Comanche, most ricky-ticky pronto," Gavich mumbled.

"What's the load?" I asked.

"Boss didn't say. He just said they want it out there bad, and best we waste no time."

"Somehow…" Roto-rooter said, hanging smoke grenades on a vertical post by his gun bay, "…I just feel in my bones, it ain't gonna be Raquel Welch and the Dallas Cowboy Cheerleaders."

"Attitude! Attitude!" I said, grinning, "Alright, let's kick the tires and light the fires and find out what's so goddamned special they need us to hurry in this awful heat." In a few minutes our homemade hurricane was thundering along a dirt taxi-way toward the division supply staging area on the far side of the airfield.

A dust-doomed private at the supply depot ran out to direct us to a loading slot, his arms raised in the air. He motioned us to a sandbag landing pad near a covered deuce-and-a-half truck. When we set down and reduced pitch, our load straggled out from behind the truck, all hunched against the blowing red dust. Four voices on the aircraft intercom simultaneously muttered, "Oooooh… shit!"

We suspiciously eyed five unthrilled looking soldiers, holding chain leashes connected to five enormous barking and thrashing German Shepherd dogs. You can see it coming, can't you? I wish I could have.

"Kiss my ass!" Moses moaned on the intercom, "One a them mutts shits on my aircraft and we're really gonna have a war!"

"Damn!" Gavich exclaimed, "They dogs, or Kodiak Brown Bears?"

"All right, all right," I said. "Sooner we lock and load 'em, sooner we get rid of 'em. Get 'em aboard, Mose."

The grunt that guided us in jumped up on the left skid and bellowed over the scream of the turbine, "Had a big firefight out at LZ Comanche last night, Sir! They think the gooks dragged off a bunch of dead bodies, and they want these dogs out there to sniff up the graves. Makes the body count look better, you know? How many you wanna take on the first load?"

I surveyed the five handlers and their animals and concluded they wouldn't be heavy enough to exceed gross weight with the fuel we carried. "Fuck it!" I Shouted. "Load 'em all! No need for a second trip!" The private gave me a 'thumbs up' and waved at the handlers who then dragged their charges forward.

Roto-rooter was peering nervously at the snarling dogs. "Uh, Sir, I don't think…"

"Hurry up!" I roared at the dog handlers over the booming rotor blast, "Let's go!"

They lined up, taking short-leash holds on the tense dogs, and Moses directed them to spots on the six-by-eight foot cargo floor. Roto-rooter extended a hand to guide one handler, studied the curled, drooling lips and 'go-to-hell' looks on the dogs and thought better of his hand. The wired dogs and their sweating handlers crowded into the confined cargo area between the gun bays in the rear and the armored backs of the cockpit seats. Gavich reached between the pilot seats to pet one of the dogs, and its handler swatted the hand down a nanosecond before his organic chainsaw ate it. "Holy shit!" Gavich said, snatching his hand back. "Jesus, Slush… I don't know about this!"

I twisted in my seat and squinted through my helmet visor at the grunts seated butt-down on the open floor between the door-less sides of the ship, each with a white knuckled choke hold on the leash chains, and each sweating like a lawyer at confession. The dogs were wide-eyed and trembling. Back in his gun bay, Moses pulled his helmet visor down over his face and took a tight, gloved grip on a spare M-60 machinegun barrel. That should have told me something.

9

I looked at the dogs again. Although I couldn't hear it for my helmet and the engine racket, it didn't take a genius to see from their twitching lips, bared gums and dripping fangs that they were growling threats at each other. It didn't take a genius to do what I did next, either. "Fuck it," I said. "They're under control. Let's rock and roll. Get us a clearance, Mike."

We hover-taxied to the linked steel plate runway and ran the checklist. Shortly, we heard, "Blackjack four-four, wind one-six-zero at ten knots... you're cleared for takeoff... straight out departure approved."

I keyed the radio, "Blackjack four-four, roger, we're on the go, straight out." I pushed the cyclic forward, pulled collective pitch, and the big Huey lumbered into the air, massively compounding the chain of errors inexorably underway.

I gave Gavich the controls and occupied myself with plotting our course away from the big airfield at Pleiku toward LZ Comanche. Then Roto-rooter's voice came over the intercom: "Mr. Slusher, permission to test the guns?" An aviation milestone was only seconds away. It was standard procedure on the first flight of the day to fire short bursts from the guns at a clear area to ensure they were in working order.

"Sure, Roto," I said, "let her rip." And with those immortal words began the first helicopter aerial dogfight in the history of the world.

Roto-rooter and Moses cranked off the first rounds, the big M-60's bucked, boomed and spewed hot brass shell casings into the cabin among the confined dogs and their handlers. The first decibel of the first shot had not even begun to fade before the dogs came to critical mass. Every nerve in every monster dog aboard blew right out the end. Simultaneously, I heard screams, raging snarls and shouts. I felt impacts jolt against the back of my seat and I noted tufts of hair and little green pieces of jungle-fatigues in the air. Right away I knew something was not entirely swell. I whipped my head around to view a scene that made Hell look like an expensive Bangkok massage parlor by comparison.

The entire interior of the aircraft was a roiling pandemonium of swirling dogs and men and cacophonous noise. The dogs, all five of them, were in the 'kill-everything-and-let-God-sort-it-out' mode, attacking anything within reach. The grunts were rolling around, clinging desperately to the chains, and either bellowing ignored commands to the animals or screaming in agony. There was blood on the dogs, blood on the handlers, and blood on the aircraft. Globs of hair and strips of green cloth blew in the turbulent air. My seat shook with the bodies bouncing off of it.

Moses was flailing wildly at anything he could hit with the spare M-60 gun-barrel. Roto-rooter was pounding dog and man indiscriminately with a folded foxhole shovel. To my additional horror, I noted two places in the overhead where the quilted soundproofing had been torn away and vital aircraft nerve lines of little colored wire were exposed. Worse, one of the tumbling dog handlers was whacking an opposing dog with his presumably loaded .45 automatic pistol. This is not what you like to see in your aircraft at two thousand feet in the air

"Oh God," Gavich said on the intercom, barely audible over the screaming, snarling, thrashing, and the thumps of impact. I spun about and seized the controls.

"I got it!" I said to Gavich, "I don't care how you do it, but you keep those dogs out of this cockpit!" I dropped the ship into a rapid descent and looked below for a safe place to land. It was about here that one of Roto-rooter's frantic slashes with the shovel snagged a smoke grenade on the fore-stroke.

A little technical background is in order here. It was common practice to hang smoke grenades from gun bay posts by their detonation rings so, that if we were fired upon, near the surface, all a crewman needed to do, in order to quickly mark the location of the enemy fire, was snatch one of the grenades off the post and throw it out the door. It would, of course, explode in three seconds as its fuse-ring remained on the doorpost. Smoke grenades don't blow-up, per se, they simply discharge copious, powder-thick clouds of vividly colored smoke designed to be seen by aircraft miles away for a solid minute. They also become hot enough to give you third degree burns. You're getting the picture.

The grenade did a 'two banker' off the ceiling and the back of Gavich's seat, and spun into the maelstrom on the cargo floor. It gave off with a loud crack, and gushed an acrid stream of sulfuric, bright-red smoke. You would think the prevailing situation couldn't have gotten any worse, but you'd be real wrong.

The world's first helicopter aerial dogfight went into hyper-drive as the scalding hot grenade hissed about among the hysterical dogs and handlers, filling the entire interior of the aircraft with a choking, blinding red cloud. On my first inhalation, my lungs slammed shut and my eyes were seared. Fortunately, I instantly recalled the emergency procedure for smoke in the cockpit; I reached down with my left hand and yanked the pilot-door jettison-handle. The door at my elbow disappeared and the smoke vented enough for me to see and breathe. Unfortunately, in my haste I neglected a vital detail of the procedure, which was to slow the aircraft to a hover before punching off the door. We were in a high-speed dive when I let mine go. It caught in the slipstream, whipped aft and smashed a deep gouge in the tail-rotor driveshaft housing on top of the tail boom, before disappearing toward the jungle below. Even over the pandemonium in the cabin behind me, I could hear the high-pitched squeal of metal grating on metal. "What's that noise?" Gavich demanded, his voice catching. He didn't have to wait long for his answer.

There was a grinding bang from the rear; the ship suddenly lurched into a right yaw and leaned over hard to the left, dumping the raging passengers toward the open left doorway. This development got the attention of the handlers, who grappled for handholds, but the dogs continued their fight to the death… they were nearer than they knew.

Moses leaned out over his gun, hacking from streams of red smoke flowing over him, and craned to see aft. "The tail-rotor… ain't turnin', Mr. Slusher!" he shouted over the intercom, breathing hard, screams and snarls in the background.

"Oh, lovely," I thought as I steered with great difficulty toward the airfield. The ship settled down to a left-forward, crab-like, flight path, while all that now kept the fuselage from rotating in the opposite direction from the main-rotor was our speed through the air. In such a situation, hovering was impossible and an airplane-style, run-on landing was the designated emergency response. I would literally skate the ship onto its skids at forty to fifty knots.

"Plei… CAHCH! …ku Tower!" I called over the radio, choking and coughing. "Blackjack… Four-Four…, CAHCH-HACH-HACH! EMERGENCY!"

"Uh, say again, Blackjack Four-Four?" the tower controller answered, no doubt puzzled at the sounds of a blazing dogfight in the background of my transmission. Then he must have caught sight of a Huey belching clouds of red smoke, approaching his airfield while flying sideways and opposite the direction of traffic. "All aircraft Pleiku, exit the runway and remain clear of the control zone… Emergency in progress!" I could see the big yellow crash wagons roar forth from their garages on the airfield ahead, red lights flashing, and crewmen donning silver fire protection suits.

A scrambling dog's ass presented itself between the armor plates of the cockpit seats. "Get that dog outa my cockpit!" I screeched at Gavich, who promptly began to beat the dog in the butt with the only available tool, his revolver. For his efforts, we were suddenly rewarded with the business end of the animal.

"AAAAAAH!!" Gavich yelled, whacking frantically at the dog's snarling, snapping head. I saw him trying to take aim.

"Don't shoot! Don't shoot!" I screamed, without benefit of the intercom. I struggled to align the ship with a shallow approach angle to the runway… I was downwind but there was no time to go around the pattern. We soared over the approach lights, and the rubber streaked touchdown zone of the runway flashed beneath us. I shut in the throttle to take the torque out of the system and let her settle onto the steel runway. The skid heels scraped plating, I reduced pitch, and the ship screeched down the runway at about forty knots, trailing clouds of red smoke and a shower of sparks. It was still sliding when Moses and Roto-rooter began hooking people and dogs out both doors with the shovel and machine-gun barrel.

The big Huey finally ground to a halt, two dogs and handlers still flailing at each other in the smoke-shrouded cargo bay. Crash trucks squealed to a stop at either side of the aircraft; moon-suited firemen bailed off and dragged foam hoses under the slowing coasting main-rotor. Moses and I both screamed "N00000!" at the same time, but it was too late. Stinking, slimy torrents of crash foam spewed forth all over everything and everybody.

The colonel commanding my aviation brigade stepped out of his jeep and surveyed several grunts, dogs and helicopter crewmen, lying or standing at various points about the runway. All were coated like drowned rats in a peculiar mixture of blood, red powder and soapy foam, some coughing and heaving for breath and some with blood-stained, torn clothing. Near the crippled, red-tinted, foam smeared helicopter, rescuers were attempting to beat back one last die-hard German Shepherd which wouldn't allow them near its handler who lay comatose on the runway.

"This," the colonel said with genuine wonder, "is the damnedest thing I ever saw."

"Yes Sir." I said, elegantly blowing red mucous onto the steel and seeing my whole aviation career flash before my eyes.

The colonel sighed. "Well, hell, there's only one thing to do now."

"Yes, Sir." I repeated. This, I was sure, was where he would rip the wings off my uniform and banish me for the duration to become sanitary landfill officer.

The colonel barked, "Mr. Slusher, you and your people go preflight another aircraft, and then get these goddamn dogs out to LZ Comanche!" He turned and strode briskly for his jeep. "And this time, no horsing around!"

ABOUT THE AUTHOR: William (Bill) Slusher served as a helicopter pilot with the 4th Aviation Battalion, 4th Infantry Division from July 1968 to March 1969. He is the author of the books "Shepherd Of The Wolves" and "Butcher Of The Noble" and lives on his horse farm in Charles Town, West Virginia.

RAINBOW CHARLIE

By Lieutenant Colonel Robert W. Michel, U.S. Army Retired

Religion was never a vital part of my adult life, even though I had had a strict Catholic upbringing and still wear a "Miraculous" medal around my neck, which was given to me by my saintly Aunt Irene when I entered the Army in 1952. An event occurred, however, mid way through my tour in Vietnam that reaffirmed my belief in the "Almighty" and the notion that, in God's eyes the value of a human soul isn't necessarily judged by whose side you're on.

It looked as though it was going to be a beautiful day that March morning in 1967. A low early morning haze blanketed the ground. Light rain showers were forecasted for the afternoon, but the sky was clear and a slight cool breeze made conditions perfect for an airmobile assault. While my memory of the exact date and names of people, especially first names, has been dimmed by time, my recollection of the events on that cool day in March will stay with me to the grave.

We had just picked up elements of an infantry company of the U.S. Army, 173rd Airborne Brigade from the soccer field in Saigon, one of the few open areas in the city that was used routinely as a helicopter staging area by U.S. and Vietnamese forces. Our mission was to take us to a cluster of rice paddies six miles east of Saigon where a Viet Cong (VC) guerrilla force of unknown size was reportedly encamped along a creek line jutting into the Saigon River.

As our flight of fourteen UH-1 (Huey) helicopters passed over the east edge of the city, I recall thinking how peaceful it appeared below in the early dawn — a few taxicabs and people on motor scooters — bicycles going about their business as street merchants set up shop for the day. It seemed absurd that such a tranquil setting could harbor hostility. Likely as not, the intelligence we had received about a large VC presence this close to Saigon was old, and by now stale, so we would encounter nothing in a sweep of the area. It wouldn't be the first time that so-called "hard intelligence" would result in nothing more than an aggravated case of athletes' foot from wading through rice paddies all day.

On final approach to the landing zone (LZ) adjacent to the creek line, I glanced to my right at the skyline of Saigon. My eyes came to rest on the Caravel Hotel, which stood out clearly among the cluster of downtown buildings. It was said that members of the news media who made up the bulk of the hotel's guest list, watched the war while dining at the rooftop restaurant. "No action today fellas," I remember saying to myself as my gaze fixed on the rooftop, "We're on a milk run."

I was flying the Command and Control (C&C) helicopter and was the senior member of our helicopter unit. On board the chopper was the Infantry Battalion S-3 (Operations Officer), a Major, and my crew consisting of co-pilot, Chief Warrant Officer Bustamonte (Busti for short), an old timer with a lot of flying experience, as well as two door gunners, Corporals Cotinno and Bagley. Cotinno, a tall, lanky kid who grew up on the Caribbean island of Jamaica was deadly accurate with an M-60 machine gun, the standard weapon used by helicopter door gunners. It was rumored that he could selectively shoot a coconut out of a palm tree from 1,000 feet in the air without disturbing the other coconuts on the tree. In his Caribbean accent he would say, "Mon" instead of "Man" and when referring to me in conversation with his buddies called me "De Boss Mon". Bagley was new to our unit, a quiet kid but very conscientious about his performance as a door gunner. I felt very comfortable with Cotinno and Bagley protecting our flanks.

The creek line ahead of us was thick with palm trees and lush tropical foliage, offering excellent concealment, if in fact VC were using it as a base camp. Between the creek line and a long stretch of rice paddies was an area of uncultivated solid ground about 50 yards from the creek that was chosen as our LZ. A handful of farmers were tilling the rice paddies. Usually, farmers would stop working and stand motionless as we approached so as not to appear threatening when alerted to our presence by the 'wop, wop, wop' of the rotor blades. Today's response was different. They all dropped their rakes and ran feverishly away from the creek line. My instincts smelled trouble and my adrenaline soared. I immediately keyed my intercom button to alert the Battalion S-3 to the situation.

"Major, I think something is up. Do you see that?" I asked pointing to the fleeing farmers.

"Yea, I see them." he replied.

"I'd like to have our gunships lay down suppressing fire along the creek line as we land."

"Negative!" he shot back. "We're in a pacified area. No shooting unless we're shot at first."

By this time, our flight of Hueys was about 50 feet in the air, seconds away from touchdown. "Keep an eye on the creek line, you guys!" I announced over the radio to our flight crews. No sooner had I spoken than the creek line came alive with gunfire. Muzzle flashes from AK-47 machine guns and other small arms were visible everywhere. The Viet Cong (VC) had caught us in our most vulnerable posture… at hover disembarking troops. The infantry, without hesitation began spilling out of the Hueys. Three troopers landed face down in the dirt, killed by gunfire before their feet touched the ground. I could see others squirming on the ground obviously hit, but still alive. The Huey door gunners facing the creek line instinctively returned fire, but it was too late to spoil the aim of the VC. Although it had only taken three to four seconds to unload the troops, I later learned that in that short time we suffered eleven casualties… five dead and six wounded. Nine of our 14 helicopters were hit by ground fire, although none seriously.

Gunfire from the creek line continued as the troop carrying Hueys lifted off to return to the soccer field and await further orders. At the same time, my unit's helicopter gunships swung to attack. With the troops on the ground pinned down behind a two-foot high dike, forward movement was impossible. The only firepower we had to support the ground troops were the door guns on my C&C helicopter and my unit's four gunships equipped with 2.75 in. rockets and machine guns.

"Bandit 36, this is Thunderbird 3," I radioed to my gunship platoon leader.

"This is Bandit 36, go ahead."

"Work over the edge of the creek line and lay it on heavy!" I radioed to the gunship.

"Roger, Thunderbird 3."

Our gunships by themselves didn't have the firepower or staying power to defeat what we now concluded was a substantially large and well dug-in VC force. "Can we get any Air Force support?" I asked the Battalion S-3.

"Tan Son Nhut airbase is only a few miles away. I'll call Battalion Headquarters and request it," he replied.

No sooner had our gunships exhausted their ammunition supply than a flight of fighter-bombers arrived and began dropping bombs on the creek line and staffing with 20-millimeter cannons. The affect was visibly devastating. Palm trees along the creek line were stripped bare by bomb fragments and concussion waves, but the infantry on the ground continued to report heavy automatic weapons fire from the creek, preventing their advance.

For the remainder of the day, into late afternoon, the bombing and strafing continued alternating between the Air Force jets and our helicopter gunships. The creek line was beginning to resemble a burned out forest. Naked, blackened tree stumps were all that remained of a once lush wooded area.

As the sun began to fade in the Western sky we were informed, via the Battalion S-3 on board, that enemy contact on the ground had ceased and that an extraction of the troops had been ordered by Battalion Headquarters. Our Hueys headed back for the evacuation from their holding position at the soccer field and medical evacuation helicopters were called in to pick up the dead and wounded.

Remembering the mission we had originally been directed to undertake, I asked the Battalion S-3, "What about letting us finish the job we started on the ground?"

"No way," he replied "Battalion Headquarters has decided to make a ground assault from a different direction using trucks and Armored Personnel Carriers (APCs). The guys on the ground below us are too shaky and demoralized to finish the job. We're taking them out."

The extraction took place without incident and as the last helicopter departed the LZ, I could sense the anger and frustration that gripped everyone onboard my chopper. We had airlifted close to 100 men on an assault, 8 miles from their home base with nothing to show for their efforts except 11 casualties. Not one foot of ground was gained nor were we able to confirm that any damage had been done to the VC. It was a bad day indeed, but not yet over.

It was customary in most aviation units for the C&C helicopter to make a low pass over an LZ once it was vacated, to visually ensure that no one was left behind by mistake. Accordingly, I proceeded to make a low pass over the LZ. It was quiet below and there was nothing on the ground except a few discarded ammunition bandoleers. As I pulled up into a steep right turn, a light rain that had been forecast began to fall from a thin layer of broken clouds. I'm not sure what prompted me to look back over my shoulder at the creek line, but as I did, I glimpsed what appeared to be the bow of a dugout canoe protruding from the remaining foliage right where the river met the creek. Within moments, the entire canoe—all 20 feet of it—was visible. Standing in the middle of the dugout was a figure in black pajamas (the typical uniform of VC guerrillas) holding a long pole that he was using to propel the dugout out into the river.

"I don't believe it!" blurting my thoughts of astonishment out over the intercom. How could that bastard have survived the blitzkrieg that descended on him all day long? By now everyone in the chopper was focused on the VC in the dugout.

"Maybe his wife told him not to be late for dinner." Busti sarcastically remarked.

"Let's see if we can make that permanent!" I added. "Cotinno, I'll drop down to 200 feet and circle over him. He's all yours."

"Okay, Boss!" Cotinno confirmed as he leveled the M-60 machine gun at the dugout and cut loose with a long uninterrupted stream of fire. The spray from bullets striking the river completely engulfed the VC until he was no longer visible through the cascade of water. Bullets struck the dugout, chipping away at it piece by piece. After what seemed an inordinate amount of time, Cotinno stopped firing. The blanket of water subsided only to reveal Charlie (the nickname given to VC guerrillas) still upright in his dugout poling his way down the river, apparently undaunted by the ferocity of our attack.

"Cotinno, what in hell's the problem? That should have been an easy shot for you!" I said in an irritated tone.

"I dunno, Boss. I should have got de' mon."

"Okay, Bagley, its your turn. I'll bank the bird to your side so you can get a clear shot at him."

"Roger, Sir." Bagley turned his M-60 on the VC with intense deliberation and a rain of bullets descended on the dugout. Like all of us, he had witnessed the carnage that had taken place on the ground earlier in the day and undoubtedly hoped to even the score if only in a token way. Again, the figure in the dugout was completely obscured by the water spray as bullets impacted the river around him. Fragments of the dugout flew in every direction. When Bagley stopped firing to let the barrel of his weapon cool, to our amazement, the VC was still standing upright in the bullet-riddled shell of his dugout—apparently unscathed! He never looked up at us or showed any sign of panic. Why he hadn't abandoned ship and tried to swim to shore from the very beginning was a mystery. A logical choice would have been to head for the shore 20 yards away and hope for concealment in the foliage along the river's edge. Instead, he seemed oblivious to our attack and somewhat complacent about his own situation.

"What's wrong, Bagley?" I barked.

"I can't explain it, Sir…" was the bewildered reply over the intercom.

"Enough of this!" I said, "From this altitude we should be able to hit the bastard with a rock. Busti… take the controls and drop down to a hover over the water. I'll take Charlie out with my sidearm."

I lowered the window next to me and unholstered my pistol as Busti made a slow descending turn to the river. At 10 feet over the water and about 100 yards from the VC, the sight before me left me in awe. From our low altitude angle of view, the dugout, which had sunk to the gunwale, was out of sight, leaving the impression that Charlie was standing on top of the water with only the pole in his left hand for support. It was reminiscent of a biblical scene I had once viewed on a stained glass window of a cathedral in Italy! The rain had ceased while we were descending and suddenly a beam of sunlight broke through the clouds and shone directly on the dugout. Simultaneously, a rainbow arched over the river framing the man standing there in a multi-spectral halo.

"Holy shit!!" said the Battalion S-3 who was sitting between Busti and myself in the jump seat of our chopper.

"Mon, will you look at dat!" Cotinno piped in.

"Weird!" was all Bagley could say, stunned by the vision.

I looked over at Bustamonte, "What do you think, Busti?"

After a moment he replied, "I think the Man upstairs is trying to tell us something."

"Yeh… " I said, holstering my sidearm. I still needed to satisfy my curiosity as to how the VC had survived our attack. "Get closer to Charlie, Busti." As we neared the dugout at a slow hover, the man in black stood motionless. His pajamas, soaked with water, clinging so tightly to his body that you could see the muscles in his arms and legs through the material. Water spilled from his coal black hair and ran over his face. The bamboo pole he used for propulsion was gouged all over from repeated bullet strikes. The submerged dugout had hundreds of punctures in it from the onslaught of bullets, and yet the man himself was untouched. Incredible, I thought, as our eyes met. His face was expressionless and as we drew near, I got the feeling that he was ready to accept his fate. When we came abreast of the dugout, ten feet or so away, I smiled at him and raised my right hand in a half-hearted salute. A smile pierced the blank expression on his face and he returned the gesture. I motioned for Busti to gain altitude and return to base camp. "Let's go home."

No one spoke during the remainder of the flight. There was no rational explanation for what had take place, but it was obvious from the silence onboard the chopper that each of us had been touched in some way by our encounter with "Rainbow Charlie."

Many years later during a chance meeting with a comrade in arms from my unit, we talked at length about our experiences in Vietnam. He had the uncanny ability to recall names, places and details that I had long since forgotten. In the course of conversation, I brought up the subject of the 173rd Airborne Brigade excursion east of Saigon, without mentioning the Rainbow Charlie encounter fearing how he might react to the thought that I believed in Divine intervention. In the middle of my monologue, he butted in with a comment which, when I think of it today, still gives me goose bumps. "You know Bob, if memory serves, we ran that operation on March 23rd, Easter Sunday."

ABOUT THE AUTHOR: Robert (Bob) Michel served with the 118th Assault Helicopter Company, 145th Aviation Battalion, 1st Aviation Brigade from October 1966 to November 1967. He died of lung cancer in early 2004 and is survived by his wife, Patti, their five children, five grandchildren, and tons of friends.

BRIAN, I HARDLY GOT TO KNOW YOU

By Captain Art Littlefield, U.S. Marine Corps, Retired

I met newly commissioned 2nd Lieutenant Brian O'Connor in October of 1966. We both joined "H" Company, 2nd Battalion, 1st Marine Regiment, at about the same time, just as the war was beginning to crank up a notch.

We were different more than we were alike. He was a practicing Irish-Catholic. I was a dropout Methodist. He was a recent college graduate, a product of the Platoon Leader Course and Marine Basic School. I was a Staff Non-Commissioned Officer with 16 years service, converted from Gunnery Sergeant to instant Second Lieutenant. He was newly married with no children. I was a 13-year married man with three children. Brian was old for his years and somewhat of an intellectual, while I was a more carefree and streetwise. We both came from the Northeast, however, and we both loved the Corps. There was instant chemistry between us.

Although we operated together on company or battalion-sized operations, we didn't see that much of each other in the bush as he was with his platoon and I was with mine. But whenever we were in company bivouac at the same time, we sought each other out to compare notes. We passed on information about areas where one of us had patrolled and the other would soon be headed, like where the Viet Cong mines were on a given path or what village to expect fire from.

As time went by, we grew painfully proficient at everything from three-man all-night listening posts to night ambushes and patrolling day and night. When not in the bush, we spent most of our time together. We rarely, if ever, talked about home. Our lives were strictly business; mines, patrols and the business of staying alive. We thought we followed the unspoken rule that it was best not to get too close, but we were close anyway and we drew strength from one another.

We shared advice about a lot of things, but neither of us had any answer for the continuing casualties. When either of our platoons took casualties, it was deeply personal - almost as though we had overlooked something we shouldn't have. On that issue, we couldn't console one another.

One day, Brain said to me. "You know we're not going to make it through this, don't you?" I sidestepped his seriousness with something glib and that was the end of it. But the impact of what he said stayed with me. Another time, he asked me "What's the next line of 'Who knows for whom the bell tolls?'" (Quoting from Hemmingway's novel). He paused and then quietly answered his own question. "It tolls for thee."

Brian's fatalism shook me. So many things were better left unsaid. And then it happened. We were on the second or third day of a battalion search-and-destroy operation deep in what the troops called Indian Country. I saw Brian go down. He had taken a round through his mid-section. As he was being loaded onto the Med-Evac chopper, he was still conscious and very vocal. Over the roar of the chopper blades, I could hear him protesting his forced departure. In shock, and unaware of the seriousness of his wound, he was furious at having to leave his men.

Normally, the chopper would have flown to the nearest aid station, but because of the nature of the wound, the pilot flew directly to Da Nang Hospital. Brian was Dead On Arrival. It was January 30, 1967. Our friendship had lasted less than four months.

But it isn't over. Brian is still with me. To this day, I feel his presence tagging along, curious to know what life might have been like, if only he'd had the chance to live it.

ABOUT THE AUTHOR: Arthur (Art) Littlefield was a platoon leader in "H" Company, 1st Marine Regiment, 1st Marine Division from October 1966 to November 1967. He resides with wife Jo in Orlando, Florida.

THE NEWBEE

By Sergeant Major George S. Kulas, U.S. Army Retired

As we were leaving the plane in Da Nang, the stewardess announced that she hoped we had a good tour, not a good day as is usually the custom. I remember thinking to myself that I probably wouldn't have a good day, or see another pretty blonde, blue-eyed woman like the stewardess for the next 13 months. Departing the air-conditioned plane the heat and humidity outside was stifling, like walking into a steam bath.

It was March 27, 1967 and I had arrived at Da Nang Air Base, South Vietnam. I was a young, green marine private. Our group of new arrivals hadn't even reached the terminal when we heard the label being placed upon us. Here come some more "newbees", short for new boys, was being yelled our way. Other comments such as, "Man are they green," "I've got 29 days and a wake up, and my replacement is here," were directed at us. I thought, how long will it take to get rid of the label of "newbee?" A week, a month, certainly after 3 months I would be just another one of the boys.

After a few days of processing, Private Jennings and I were sent to Communications Company, Headquarters, 3rd Marine Division at Phu Bai. I was relieved not to have to report in alone; I wouldn't be the solo newbee arriving in the unit. Since we both hadn't yet received our security clearance, we were placed on an outside work detail for the communications center, where we would eventually work, but for the present, were not allowed to enter.

Master Gunnery Sergeant Fairchild, the senior enlisted soldier in the communications center, traditionally referred to as "Top", promptly put us to work replacing sandbags around the communications center. We labored feverishly under the watchful eye of top Fairchild, who would pop out of the air conditioned communications center now and then to see how we were doing in the 100 degree heat and stifling humidity. After about a week the job was nearly finished, and top Fairchild seemed very satisfied with our work. He told us he was proud of the way we worked without complaining. He also told us our clearances had been granted and, when the project was completed we would be reporting to work in the communications center. We were ecstatic over the news that we would be getting out of the heat and into the cool communications center.

The next morning we reported to work to put the finishing touches on our project and encountered top Fairchild with a grim look on his face. He told us the Colonel did not like the walls, especially the way the sandbags looked. Many were filled inside out leaving a ragged appearance. The Colonel wanted them replaced.

Jennings and I knew we had filled many bags inside out, believing they would provide just as much protection filled inside out or otherwise. Many of the inside out bags were spread throughout the protective walls, which meant Jennings and I had to tear the walls down, fix the problem, and then rebuild the walls. We vocally expressed our dissatisfaction with the situation as we emptied and refilled each bag. Several days later we began working in the communications center, ribbed by our fellow marines about our farcical escapade. Typical newbees they proclaimed.

Then things went from bad to worse. "Once a marine, always a marine", is a term that is used often by marines and ex-marines. Another phrase often used to define marines who seem to do everything wrong is, "Once a shit bird, always a shit bird." This disparaging saying was now being used by other marines in the unit to describe Jennings and myself. I was determined to get rid of this description. For the next several weeks I worked hard at my new job, and was gradually gaining the respect of my superiors and peers.

Early one morning after getting off of the 1400-0200 hours shift, I was awakened around 0500 hours by voices I soon recognized as those of Sergeant Fairchild and the First Sergeant. As the voices drew closer I hear Fairchild say, "Kulas and Jennings are the newest members of the company and they'll adjust the easiest."

I was thinking, adjust to what? A few minutes later I was packing my bags, having been reassigned to the communications center at Dong Ha. I knew Dong Ha was the most northern base in South Vietnam and wasn't looking forward to going there.

At our new station we were met by a corporal who took us to see the Gunnery Sergeant (gunny for short). The gunny told us to stash our gear, get some chow, and to report for work at 2200 hours for the 2200-1000 hours shift. Explaining that we had been on duty the day and night before, and had been awake since 0500 hours, I pleaded with him to let us get some sleep, since it was now 2100 hours. The gunny, after talking with the captain, stated that Jennings would go on day shift, and I would report to his shift in one hour, no questions asked. Here I was, a newbee again getting the short end of the stick. It didn't take long, however, for me to become acclimated to the job, and the corporal training me felt comfortable leaving me on my own. By this time I was very sleepy, and began to doze off, only to be jolted awake by the gunny slamming his fist on my desk. He glared at me with his bulging eyes saying, "Marine, wake up and get to work." Snapping to, I started back at my tasks. But the need for sleep kept taking priority over my boring job, and I dozed off again and again only to be caught each time by the gunny, who was by this time short on patience with me. During one of my napping periods I was awakened by the deafening sound of shooo-boom, shooo-boom, shooo-boom! Marines were yelling, "Incoming", and diving for the deck.

I dove with them, shaking and scared. Finally the firing stopped, and we went back to work. Several minutes later the roar of boom, boom, boom, was heard. Learning my lesson from the previous sound of gunfire I screamed, "Incoming", and dove once again for the deck. As I lay there I became curious why I hadn't heard or seen any of my fellow marines yelling and diving for cover. Peeping up I saw the gunny standing over me and the other marines staring at me in disbelief. With the booming sounds still thundering I yelled, "Get down, incoming." The gunny glaring at me bellowed, "Get up marine, outgoing." After that the shift seemed to go on forever, although I was now thoroughly awake and did not doze off again.

When it did finally end, I headed straight for my tent, thinking that again I was a newbee and now a total shit bird in the eyes of my gunny and fellow marines. I knew it would take a great deal of time and effort for me to gain the confidence of everyone in the group.

The sides of the tent were rolled up to allow what breeze there was to flow freely through it. I stripped down to my underwear and went to sleep, only to awake to a searing pain in my feet. Looking at my bright red feet in horror I realized that while sleeping I had extended them out through the raised sides of the tent and they had gotten severely sun burned. Putting my socks on was extremely painful. Somehow I got my boots on, but had to lace them loosely. When I went limping to work I was more pained by the sight of the gunny outside the communications center watching me approach, than by the rubbing of the boots against my tender feet. When the gunny asked me what was wrong now, I could only tell him that I had blisters on my feet. Looking at me in a mixture of bewilderment and disgust, he said, "Kulas, it's going to be a very, very long tour for you."

It took months to work my way off the gunny's information shit bird list, and all the while I had that newbee feeling. Just when I was again gaining the respect and confidence of the gunny and my fellow marines I would screw something up.

I was assigned to make a daily round trip message courier run from Dong Ha to Quang Tri. One afternoon as I was pulling into the communications center area after returning from a trip to Quang Tri, the gunny motioned to me to park the jeep next to a formation of about 30 marines that he was addressing. As I was watching the gunny direct me, I wasn't paying attention to where I was driving.

The jeep jolted to a stop. Still looking at the gunny, whose expression changed from a helpful one to one of horror and dismay, I realized that I had run into the communications center, causing substantial damage to the structure. Now I was definitely and permanently on the list with no erasure possible.

The gunny finally completed his tour and shipped out to the states. I, now known as "clutch" by my fellow marines, had 10 months in Vietnam and decided to voluntarily extend my 13-month tour another 6 months. I did this for many reasons, but I think in the back of my mind I wanted to start over with a clean slate. I started feeling good about myself, I hadn't screwed up under a new gunny, was promoted, and worked in a supervisory position. A few months later I took my extension leave and returned to Vietnam revitalized and ready to continue doing well. The night I returned I went immediately to the hooch to sleep. My gear had been put in storage before I went on leave, so I didn't have a place to bunk down. I took the nearest bed and flopped in it. I was awakened by the marines returning from their shift later in the evening, and soon realized that I was no longer a newbee and a shit bird in the minds of my fellow marines. A marine who had arrived while I was on leave bellowed out, "There's a newbee sleeping in my bunk." Another marine who recognized me said, "That's not a newbee, you're a newbee, that's clutch, an old timer back from his extended tour; leave him alone!" I now had gained the respect I deserved.

Five months later I left Vietnam, a tired, hardened, battletested marine. My new assignment was the communications center at Camp Courtney, Okinawa. The majority of marines there had not yet been to Vietnam. So I felt it would be easy for me to fit in. I wouldn't have to take anything from anyone. When I arrived at the in-processing station on Okinawa, campaign ribbons gleaming on my chest, I proudly told the sergeant in charge that I was reporting in from Nam. He turned to a private near him and without showing any sign of recognition of my status as a Vietnam Veteran, said, "Process this newbee, he just got in."

ABOUT THE AUTHOR: George Kulas served as a communications NCO with the 3rd Marine Division from March 1967 to December 1968. He transferred to the Army in 1972 and now resides in Fond du Lac, Wisconsin with his wife Kathy.

TIGER PAUSE

By Lieutenant Colonel Richard Tokarz, U.S.A.F.
Retired

The closest I ever came to being a Tactical Air Command (TAC) fighter pilot was having a jar of hemorrhoid ointment in the medicine chest. For ten years, hot in-flight meals, plush reclining seats, walk-in latrines, autopilots, and the stress relieving crew bunks of a tanker aircraft had spoiled me.

In 1968 my idyllic career as a tanker pilot came to an end. The manpower demands of Southeast Asia could no longer be ignored, not even by the Air Force's premier peacekeepers, and the lives of thousands of airmen would be changed forever.

So it was in June that eleven other Strategic Air Command (SAC) pilots and I reported to Bergstrom Air Force Base, Texas. We were there to learn the craft of tactical reconnaissance as plied in the RF-4C Phantom fighter aircraft. After a salutary run through ground school, we got down to the business of fondling the machine. The daunting and hazardous task of checking me out in the Air Force's hottest aircraft fell to a weathered and laconic Major who I shall call Neat O. Guy, or Nog for short.

Nog plastered my flight suit to my back during high "G" force maneuvers every time we flew, but he was an excellent instructor and a natural flyer. However, like a football lineman who had hit the tackling dummy one too many times, he had some quirks. For example, after demonstrating a maneuver he would say "That was smooth, hey?" or "Man, this one worked out great!" Then he would say "Neat-O." He also had a nasty way of rebutting my best efforts with "What was that?" "Marginal." and the unkindest cut of all, "Adequate, but not up to TAC fighter pilot standards." Let's face it… the last thing a man needs to do after age thirty is join a motorcycle gang or become a fighter pilot! Nevertheless, I enjoyed flying with

31

Nog. As a stick-and-rudder man he was slicker than a new bride's thighs.

As for Nog's background, he began his career as an F-86 pilot. In Korea he had been in real dogfights and actually hit a couple of MIGs. During these engagements no enemy pilot ever got to shoot at him or his flight leader, which is a reflection of his skill. Nog also instructed in Air Force Training Command for three years and survived numerous attempts on his life by a score of eager students. Lastly, he completed a combat tour in RF-4s in Vietnam. With such impressive credentials who could expect him to make a serious judgmental error?

Segue now to the pristine blue skies of west Texas, c. 1968. We are at twenty-odd thousand feet over picturesque Crockett County, and I have just lost control of the airplane. Somehow in an attempt at making a vertical recovery I ham-fist the bird into what I at first think is a spin. However, when I look out for references there is no rotating topography to confirm this notion. Instead there is a recurring flash of blue/brown, and we seem to be tumbling end-over-end like a banana. The counter drum pointer on the altimeter slows its upward movement, stops, and then reverses. Soon we will be dropping like the Cubs in a pennant race! OK, this is not one of my better days, but I am not completely responsible for getting us into this predicament, either.

Nog is a smoker. He carries a tin Band-Aid box in the pocket of his G-suit that he uses as an ashtray. Halfway through a Cuban Eight he announces that he is going "cold mike" to burn one. "Just keep playing with the bird," he says, matter-of-factly.

The altimeter is unwinding rapidly, but there is no reaction from the rear cockpit. Is Nog in shock... finishing his cigarette? More than likely he's simply demonstrating the fabled sang-froid of the breed.

The airplane is in limbo, its controls useless at the moment. Something must be done lest we wind up ankle-deep in rattlesnakes, but what? I recall a training film in which a company test pilot recommends letting go of everything and deploying the drag chute which is a sixteen-foot diameter slotted nylon airbrake normally used for slowing the aircraft after landing. It takes a lot of willpower to release the stick, because in a wildly gyrating aircraft it is the staff of life. I do so, however, and pull upon the yellow handle between the seat and the left console. It doesn't appear to be helping matters. Then the nose of the Phantom arcs through the horizon toward the waiting sagebrush. It slices through the vertical, pauses, then swings back and stabilizes. The airspeed indicator springs to life. I grasp the stick and can feel a slight stiffening as the airspeed builds. I ease the throttles forward in pursuit of the needle, and we are back in business about twelve thousand feet above the terrain. The stabilator leading edge is itching for a bite of air, but hey! Why not seize the moment to give 'ol Nog a thrill? I push the power up to full mil without making an attempt to recover. C'mon Nog - where are ya? I apply backpressure, but the stick seems frozen. I try both hands. Nothing! I pull harder, motivated by visions of fireballs and coyote meat.

Suddenly the intercom crackles and Nog has the bird. Then my buttocks spread like oleo on the seat cushion and my torso is crushed like a fat man's arch supports. I black out.

When I revive we are in a slight climb and Nog tells me to jettison the drag chute. We level off on an easterly course and Nog begins to hum - a sign that he is in a good mood! At last he has enough on me to put me up before a Flying Evaluation Board. We get a radar directed straight-in approach to the home drome and the mobile controller transmits "no chute" over and over until we clear the runway.

I expect a harsh critique, but Nog is subdued and affable as he recaps the mission. I wait for the ax to fall, but he just smiles and says, "I hope you learned from the experience." I ask about the lost drag cute and he dismisses it as a consequence of its natural function of saving our hides.

My attempt at hustling Nog had backfired badly, and he turned the tables on me big time. My temporary lapse into madness was not enough to elevate me into the brotherhood, but the episode proved to be a watershed in our professional relationship. His condescending manner disappeared and he never called me a "SAC Weenie" again.

Even if I never became a TAC fighter pilot, I had crossed the Rubicon and couldn't go back from whence I came.

It has been twenty-five years since I tried to run a squirrel up Nog's leg, and the world has changed dramatically. Nog went "cold mike" permanently four years ago, and I have interviewed at the Social Security office. The Phantom soldiers on as though we never existed, and the redoubtable "double ugly" tanker may outlive everybody.

The two Air Force commands TAC and SAC that grew Nog and I into aviators with irreconcilable differences have been dissolved, reformed and merged into a new entity, The Air Combat Command (ACC). Amazingly, some of the hot new jet jockeys assigned to fighter squadrons today wear bras and pantyhose... 0 Tempora! 0 Mores!

ABOUT THE AUTHOR: Richard (Dick) Tokarz was based in Udorn, Thailand, and flew 176 combat missions over Vietnam as a reconnaissance pilot with the 432nd Tactical Reconnaissance Wing (1968-69). He resides in Yorktown, Virginia with his wife Mary.

INCIDENCE OR COINCIDENCE

By Lieutenant Colonel Ralph Baber, U.S.A.F. Retired

Over forty years have gone by since I graduated from Georgia Tech. I shall never forget our school colors, white and gold. One of our Georgia Tech legends was George P. Burdell, a fictional character created by World War II veterans who attended the university on the GI Bill, older guys experienced in performing acts of chicanery. George, the fictive student, registered, attended classes, and took tests. According to a university publication, his crowning achievement, perhaps, came at graduation when a testy voice announced over the loudspeaker that "George P. Burdell would not be allowed to march with the rest of his class if he didn't pick up his cap and gown within the next fifteen minutes."

George P. Burdell later became a Vietnam veteran. He was a U-10 aircraft pilot at Pleiku in the central highlands. Although he was at Pleiku for only a few days, George made an inestimable contribution to the war effort. Well, perhaps I exaggerate a bit when I say war effort. What he really did was make life more tolerable for four U-10 pilots and three weather officers.

The seven of us shared a barracks or "hooch" intended to house 20 people. It was a single building, about 20 feet wide and nearly 60 feet long, without any interior walls. When it first was designated sleeping quarters, there were 20 GI bunks installed with a double metal locker between each bunk, a very crowded arrangement indeed. A small writing table and chair completed the individual furnishings. By placing the lockers, however, on one side of the six by eight space, you could achieve a modicum of privacy, a commodity in short supply in the military.

When I arrived as an FNG (Fucking New Guy), the FOGs (Fucking Old Guys) had rearranged the furniture, fabricated hanging lamps, and used midnight-requisitioned plywood to partition off a bar and lounge area in the front of the hooch. The remainder of it had been remodeled so each of us had a considerably larger "private space" than had been originally planned for. Two of the smaller spaces were kept intact for overnight visitors.

We lived in relative luxury until… until…

The newly assigned housing officer arrived, a brand-new, gold-bar, Second Lieutenant. He was a still wet-behind-the-ears ROTC graduate. We heard a rumor that he would soon inventory the available sleeping spaces in the compound. Hurriedly we executed Contingency Plan A that was to rearrange our hooch to appear as if it housed 20 men instead of seven. We put sheets and blankets on the extra bunks, put shoes and boots under them, and put nametapes on the lockers. I put "George P. Burdell, Major" on one of them.

A few days later the new lieutenant made his inspection. He carefully recorded that we had twenty spaces in a twenty-man facility, all apparently occupied. He paused only once, in front of Burdell's locker.

"Burdell," he muttered. "That name's familiar."

I broke in nervously. "He and I went to college together. Georgia Tech."

"Georgia Tech," he repeated as he looked me fully in the face. "I see…."

He left, we returned our quarters to their former spacious conditions, and we were not bothered during the remainder of my tour. We rejoiced in the thought that we had really put one over on the housing officer.

That's why I can say that Major Burdell, USAF, made a major contribution to the Vietnam war effort, or so we believed.

The day I left Pleiku, I checked out with the billeting office. The lieutenant saw me at the front desk, came from his office to shake hands and bid me farewell. As he went out the front door, he smiled and said, "If you see Major Burdell, tell him hello for me."

It was then I looked into his office. On the wall behind his desk was a large gold pennant emblazoned with white letters that shouted, "Georgia Tech, Class of '64."

ABOUT THE AUTHOR: Ralph Baber commanded a detachment of U-10 (psychological operations) aircraft from May 1966 to May 1967. He resides in Tow, Texas with his wife Clara.

STEPHEN T. SMITH, COMBAT MEDIC
By Michael Kelley

Sp4, Stephen T. 'Doc Smitty', Smith - Indianapolis, Indiana HHC, 1st/502d Infantry, 101st Airborne Division. Attached to 3rd Platoon, D Company, 1st/502d, Infantry Wounded 16 SEPT 70, Died of Wounds 21 SEPT 70

Doc Smitty was the last of three medics attached to the 3rd Platoon during my tenure with Delta Company, 1st Battalion 502d Infantry, between November 1969, and September 1970.

To the best of my knowledge, he was assigned to us in the spring or early summer of 1970. Steve was proud to call Indianapolis his home and liked to engage anyone he could in animated conversation about a red, 1965, Pontiac GTO, lovingly stored in the Smith family garage awaiting his return. Naturally, he was an Indy 500 fan as well and delighted in regaling us with images of the Brickyard's history of speed and his daring imitations thereof. Never at loss for words, he was eager to exercise his gift for gab any time the opportunity presented itself, whether during breaks along the trail or at our night positions. I recall him telling us that he was the only adopted son of an elderly couple who were already in their seventies when he'd left for Vietnam.

As far as I know, he was a Conscientious Objector and don't have a memory of him ever carrying any weapons except, perhaps, a 45 caliber pistol and then only as protection for his patients. Doc was about six feet tall, slender, rarely anything but cheerful and prone to embellish his stories so much so that many of us took anything be said with a generous pinch of salt. Seems we were all prone to bending the truth now and then but it wasn't normally considered as a major character flaw within our rather motley crew. The '65 GTO may have even been a fiction but it was the kind of dream we were hanging the future on and we all overlooked his possible liberties with the truth simply because those dreams were all that kept us in touch with the reality of our distant and cherished homes. He wore glasses, combed dark, straight hair and was sporting a thin mustache at the time of his death. A vague memory of a slight lisp in his speech sticks with me as well, although I'm not certain of that.

I remember him performing well when we took some non-hostile casualties in late August 1970. We were working a steep and very slippery, boulder-strewn creek bed when two of our men fell and were moderately injured. One, Beanie Wright, suffered a head injury and the other, Norman McCormick, a cracked sternum. There were no landing zones (LZ's) within reach and our mission would have been jeopardized if we were forced to carry them overland so both men had to be extracted by a medical evacuation (med-evac) helicopter, hovering high in the air above the jungle canopy. A basket was dropped for Wright and later a jungle penetrator for McCormack.

It was an exceptionally dangerous extraction. Because of the heavy jungle, the helicopter's crew had great difficulty locating our unit on the steep slope of the mountain and was forced to hover the chopper very high in the air for what seemed like an eternity until we were spotted. Smitty took care of our two friends and got them out in one piece, although most of the credit belongs to the limitless skill and courage of that med-evac crew.

Another, example of Smitty's unselfishness comes to mind that occurred while we were patrolling an area south of Firebase Arsenal, in June 1970. We were crawling on all fours through a sweltering tunnel of thick brush lined with the infamous and unmerciful 'wait-a-minute' vines common to Vietnam, when our point man blundered into a hornet's nest and literally got the hell stung out of him. Doc quickly scooted into the thicket, grabbed the trooper by the boots and unceremoniously dragged the hollering victim out of the hornet's kill zone In the process, however, Doc managed to agitate more than a few hornets himself and was soon sporting the welts of dozens of his tormentors In short order, each of our hapless pin cushions was advising us of their alleged allergy to bee venom, although we thought we could detect a lack of conviction in the announcements. As an unfortunate result, and despite our skepticism, we had little choice but to reveal our position to the enemy by calling in a med-evac helicopter and continue the mission absent the benefit of a medic for the following week. In the final analysis, neither casualty suffered much more discomfort than a few days rest in the air-conditioned luxury of the 85th Evacuation Hospital, a circumstance which prompted no small amount of grumbling speculation that they were little more than malingerers snapping up some major ghost time at our expense. Our jealousy of those whom we suspected might be getting away with more than we were, simply knew no bounds!

During the last week of August 1970, our entire battalion was airlifted to an abandoned firebase known as 'Brick', some twenty-five klicks (slang for kilometers) south of the city of Hue. Immediately preceding our early morning assault, two helicopters, scouting the advance of our insertion, had been picked out of the air by North Vietnamese Army (NVA) machine guns and their ominous wreckage littered the edges of the Landing Zone as we arrived. From then on elements of the battalion bumped into Charlie and his boys almost every day. The war had been a walk in the sun for most of my tour but things changed in a hurry after we re-opened Brick.

Firebase Brick was perched atop a huge, convoluted mountain mass about eight klicks south of our assigned area of operation (AO) and I recall watching F-4 Phantoms bomb and napalm it for days prior to our being told we would be paying the same hill a personal visit. As we watched the ongoing spectacle, in reverent awe, from the safety of our remote sanctuary, many of us expressed sincere pity for whatever unit might have been involved, friend or foe, in the action unfolding in that distant hell.

The day before our scheduled assault, new maps were flown in along with encrypted grid coordinates of our mysterious objective. Upon unshackling the coded grid and plotting the objective on the unfamiliar map, we were astonished to discover that we were to become the unit we'd pitied! It rattled some of us greatly.

As soon as the Company was dropped in, we saddled up and headed down an eastern finger of the mountain. For many days we explored the east and northeastern ridgelines of that hill mass and practically every day we encountered obvious signs that we were definitely on Charlie's home turf. Abandoned bunker complexes and supply caches were found with unsettling regularity, and enemy scouts and trail watchers were observed shadowing our daily movements.

While bivouacked as a full Company on the evening of 15 September, an NVA soldier was spotted as he scouted out our night defensive position (NDP). As a consequence a three-man dog team was brought in to track his movement in the hope he would lead us to the enemy's main body. It was a painfully slow search that tried our patience with the pampered tracker's exaggerated stealth and after several hours of fruitless searching were shocked by the dog team leader's sheepish confession that dogs were of little use in mountainous terrain because cool air took the scent down slope much too rapidly. At that point a few of us entertained the pleasant thought of putting a few rounds through the messenger. When it came time for the Company to begin moving later that afternoon, the chopper scheduled to pick up the ineffective dog team was delayed such that our platoon was required to separate from the Company in order to set up security for the dog team's eventual extraction later that evening. By the time we'd seen the team off, it was much too late for us to rejoin the other two platoons, which by then were some two klicks from our position. As an alternative, we cut a trail which took us a few hundred meters away from the LZ set up a platoon NDP, then settled in to await the dawns early light and contemplate the upcoming pleasures associated with a pending stand down at our home base in Phu Bai.

Our Company was scheduled for extraction in two days and it struck us that it would make good sense for our platoon to be picked up from the LZ which we'd secured for the dog team's extraction, rather than walk all the next morning just to catch up with the rest of Delta company. It made a lot of sense to us but none to Captain Rader our company commander. The Captain, of course, was absolutely right and he denied our request out of hand. The LZ we were hoping to use was most likely under enemy observation and potentially lethal to any American foolish enough to reuse it. Still, we made several attempts to change his mind because it would save us a long, hot walk but he refused to bend to our elaborate excuses. As fate would have it, Smitty and I would pay a heavy price for the captain's good judgment.

The next morning we started following the obvious trail left earlier by our sister platoons. After a relatively easy march, we met them along a beautiful, stony creek that reminded me much of a stream I'd fished as a child north of Montreal, Canada. We stopped, bathed under the luxurious, cool spray of natural waterfall formed by the rapidly descending creek bed and then filled both our canteens and our bellies; it provided an incredibly refreshing and welcomed break from the normal routine. The well rested and rejuvenated Company then veered off the pathway bordering the creek and started busting trail up the hill that was to be our extraction point the following morning. At the hill's base we found ourselves meandering through a heavily fortified bunker complex that had obviously been the scene of a recent and contentious fight. It was an eerie place and should have alerted us to the probability that the enemy would be foolish not to defend a potential landing zone that sat atop the hill they were using as their base of operations.

Blind to the warning, we staggered and chopped our way up the steep slope, cresting it finally in the late afternoon. It was a hot, difficult climb, and we were exhausted and soaked with sweat by the time we'd reached our objective. After a short break (during which I ate a can of pineapple bits), I had my squad begin setting up for the night. The first order of business was to put out a ring of trip flares and claymore mines that would serve as our initial line of defense against any uninvited guests.

I was teaching a new squad-member (a red-headed kid that had only been in-country a few days; think his name was Hopson) how to deploy his claymore and was instructing him to inspect every future defensive array to ensure the job had been done right, when I heard Smitty call my name from somewhere over my left shoulder. I turned to greet him but was puzzled to discover that he wasn't where his voice suggested he should have been. The small clearing was empty and it confused me greatly. At the same instant, it seemed as though someone had taken a handful of dirt and lightly tossed it into my face "What sort of idiot would pull such a stupid practical joke?" was the first thought flashing through my mind.

Nothing made much sense at that point. I had not heard any explosion (both of my eardrums had been ruptured by the blast) and it wasn't until I got the first whiff of the cordite that I began to fathom the magnitude of my predicament. My right hand tried to brush the perceived dirt from my forehead and felt what I thought to be the small, perfectly round pellets common to the construction of the claymore mine. "Oh shit," I thought, "a claymore has cooked off!" And in that instant, I knew I was about to die. I was a dead man, no ifs ands or buts about it.

I turned back to Hopson, only to find him standing as if frozen, staring at me with his mouth wide open in shock. He does not move to help, nor does anyone else. I'm baffled that no one reaches out as I stand there like a drunkard whose staggering challenge to an indifferent barroom crowd goes unanswered. The source of his horror soon became apparent as my gaze fell to my own torso. I found myself transfixed by the oddly copper-colored streams of blood that were cascading from my head, chest and stomach in almost perfect, parallel arches to the jungle's floor. There was not so much as a twinge of pain and it was difficult to distinguish between reality and the surreal nature of the bizarre landscape that was unfolding before my eyes, yet I was certain that I was about to die. It seemed I should be lying down so I went to my knees, slid over to Thyack, another one of my squad members, and simply waited for the lights to go out. I felt separated from it all, as if out of body, hovering above our remote clearing, a detached spectator. I recall a great calm washing over me, as though I'd reached the end of a long journey and the scene took on a curiously pleasant and familiar feeling. The gentle floating was soon interrupted by a wave of profound sadness as thoughts of how the news of my passing would soon savage the family so patiently awaiting my return. There was not, oddly enough, as much as a stitch of physical pain or fear.

Many faces began parading in and out of the narrowing tunnel of light through which my eyes focused on the vividly beautiful, green and gold, shimmering canopy above my resting place. I recall one face belonging to a medic from our sister platoon and it was ashen with fright and shock. He struggled to start an IV in either arm but was unsuccessful. His fear and shock were palpable and I remember feeling great pity for the self-doubt his failing would most certainly bring him. At that point, I was later told, he was replaced with the medic from yet another platoon. I hope the first medic was able to overcome the guilt and sense of failure that day may have visited upon him. He did his best for me and I wish I could thank him for trying.

Unbeknownst to me, Doc Smitty's unfortunate step had found a rather large mine. The resulting blast threw Doc at least 30 feet into the air and slammed him backside into the massive trunk of an ancient Teak that had guarded the fateful clearing for centuries. His shattered body slid down the tree's trunk, finally coming to a crumpled rest among its fluted roots, awkwardly sitting up and facing out in an almost natural pose. He was so blackened with dirt and the scorching heat of the blast that no one was really sure of his identity. A good friend of mine, Ron Johnson, recalls our platoon leader, Kenneth South of Monument Colorado, cradling the anonymous, unrecognizable, broken body gently in his arms, tears streaming down his cheeks, while he screamed for Doc Smitty's help. When the men finally lifted him to a stretcher, Ron shudders with the memory that Doc's legs felt like mush, as though the bones had been liquefied.

Smitty's good friend, Howard "Chico" Mikkali, later told me another tragic aspect of the story. Chico was the platoon leader's radioman (RTO) and Doc was the platoon medic. It was customary for both of them to sleep at the platoon's command post with the platoon leader, who was typically in the center of and controlling our night defensive positions. Because of that lofty status, both were normally exempted from the drudgeries of setting up our NDP's and that day was no exception. While the rest of us set our mines out that evening, Chico and Doc decided to play two-handed Spades but discovered that neither of them had a deck of cards at hand. Exhausted from the trek up the hill, they negotiated a flip of the coin to decide which of them would wander through the position in order to bum a deck off one of the riflemen. Smitty lost the flip, struggled to his feet and disappeared into the brush never to play cards again. Ultimately Chico lost as well, because I doubt he will ever recover from the guilt of that coin toss and the 'what ifs' of the moment.

After fashioning a litter from branches and ponchos, my panicked comrades struggled me through and around the tangled brush leading to the hastily prepared landing zone. I simply assumed that I was the only man injured. We passed a group of soldiers hunched over heating their C-rations with heat tabs and I gave a moments thought to waving good bye but stifled the impulse when I thought of how the memory of a dying man waving his last good-bye might spook them. Soon after reaching the clearing, we were met by the heavenly sounds of the med-evac helicopter frantically thumping its way through the purple-crimson edged evening sky and toward our position. With that sound came the first glimmer of hope that I might survive the day.

The med-evac landed and I was unceremoniously thrown on its diamond-patterned, cool metal floor, then, to my surprise, left alone with my garbled thoughts. The helicopter just sat there and it was my perception that no one was paying even the slightest attention to me… "What the hell is going on?" I thought, "let's get this damn thing moving!"

Suddenly there was a flurry of activity during which someone was loaded in the litter above me. I had no idea who or what it was and I'm not even sure I cared at that point; I just wanted to get the show on the road. At last we were airborne and after perhaps a ten minute, red line, balls-to-the-wall flight, flared into the landing pad adjacent to the emergency entrance of the 85th Evac, hospital at Phu Bai (the 85`` was located along the runway of Phu Bai Air Base, some five miles south of Hue). I'd once delivered mail to the very same emergency room and recall reflecting on that irony during my break-neck gurney ride through its swinging doors.

During the flight, the two medics gave the man above me their entire attention, which baffled me, some. I was finding it harder and harder to breathe (shrapnel had perforated both lungs) and finally decided it was prudent to yank at one of the green, jungle fatigued pant legs brushing against my face. A helmeted medic bent quickly to my urgent pulling and asked me what was wrong. Once apprised of my difficulty, he scavenged among the debris littering the Huey's floor and came back with a small, green oxygen bottle and its integral mask. "Hold this to your face," he told me. "The guy up here is in bad shape, and we need to work on him." With the realization borne by that simple phrase, it finally dawned on me that maybe there was a good chance I would survive the day. It is with some guilt that I recall the relief that news brought with it and that Smitty's suffering served to bring me hope, although I didn't know it was him above me at the time

In the emergency room, the med-evac scenario was repeated. The "other guy" was in a litter off to my left and he had at least six people hovering over him, while I was left with a lone orderly who kept asking me what seemed to be a series of incredibly dumb questions: What's your name? Do you want us to notify your family? About all I could think was, "Are you out of your fucking mind? Let's get this little boy into surgery ASAP and cool it with these damned silly questions!"

I woke up in the intensive care ward some hours later. I have no idea how much later or whether it was day or night. At the end of my bed were an orderly and a nurse casually discussing the fact that Jimmy Hendrix, the famous baseball player, had just died. Jimmy Hendrix was dead? I simply couldn't believe my ears. The scene was so surreal that for a few moments I actually thought I was dead and had been delivered to the gates of hell.

It was a long time, I mean hours and hours after I woke up, before they wheeled Smitty into Intensive Care, and I finally realized just who the "other guy" was. They put his bed next to mine and to my right, with perhaps ten feet separating us. Doc was a mess. Below the waist he was little more than human wreckage, pure hamburger. Above the waist, excepting his hands, not a single wound was visible. Both legs had been removed above the knees and his genitals were history too, as was a good part of both hands. Huge, green, baby diaper-like pads were wrapped around each stump and they seemed to fill with blood every few minutes. The nurses kept pumping unit after unit of blood into the poor bastard but it just seemed to he going in one end and out the other at the same speed. I don't remember any time during the next few days that someone wasn't working on him in one way or another.

Through it all, Smitty kept giving encouragement to me, sometimes in an almost breathless voice and others as if he were uninjured. "Don't worry Kelley, we'll be OK. "I could only nod and mumble in return. Tubes protruded from every orifice of my body, so mumbling and nodding was the best I could do. Although I probably looked like hell, I recall very little pain at all. In fact, I felt fine and it was Smitty who, to me, looked like death warmed over. Yet there he was trying to bolster my spirits. It was very exasperating and heartrending, and I avoided looking his way as much to avoid attracting his attention as to avoid the horror of his condition.

On the morning of 21 SEPT, they told me Doc's kidneys had failed and that he would be flown to the 3rd Field Hospital, Saigon, where I recall them saying was the only Dialysis unit in Vietnam (It still strikes me as odd that after six years of combat, there was only one Dialysis unit available in all of Vietnam). They bundled him up and took him to the plane on the nearby runway. My memory is very vague as to whether he was conscious at the time, but I have no memory of our saying good-bye to one another and would guess that he was not awake.

Some hours later a nurse came up to me and quietly told me that Smitty had died during the flight. There were tears in her eyes. As my own eyes began welling with tears of grief and loneliness, I simply told her I was glad he had died and that his suffering had come to an end. She thought about what I'd said for a moment, reached out for my hand and told me that she understood what I'd meant.

Doc Smitty died selflessly, his only apparent concern for my welfare. He died without complaint, fighting valiantly for the life he so treasured to the very end. I can only pray that my own death will be marked by such courage and such compassion for my fellow man. In the fall of 1971, Smitty's parents drove out to Sacramento from Indianapolis, for the purpose of meeting the man who was at their son's side during those last days of his short life. A very nervous and anxious me met them in their 16th Street, Sacramento, motel room one sunny, fall afternoon. They were in their seventies and the kind, gentle people who Smitty had told us about. All they wanted to ask was how Doc had died. I had sworn to myself that I would tell them the truth and nervously related every detail I could think of over perhaps a fifteen-minute period. The anxiety of the telling grew steadily as my story progressed until it simply overwhelmed me and I broke and fled the room in panic. I never saw or heard from them again and my abandonment of them in their moment of need remains one of the great regrets of my life.

ABOUT THE AUTHOR: Mike (Machine Gun) Kelly served with "D" Company, 1st Battalion, 502nd. Infantry Regiment,101st Airborne Division from November 1969 to September 1970. Am accomplished artist, he resides with his Cathryn in Sacramento, California.

THE HOSTAGE

By Commander Ralph W. Judd, U.S.C.G. Retired

On 2 February 1965 Gustav Hertz went for a ride on his motorbike through the streets of Saigon. He had made these fun trips many times before, but this one was different—he didn't return.

Hertz was an official of the U.S. Agency for International Development who, reportedly, had seen the secret plans for pacifying South Vietnam and so would be a rich prize for the Viet Cong. His wife Nellie alerted the Military Police immediately, but there were no leads to follow. As hours turned to days, she waited anxiously. Finally on 12 February the ordinary mail brought her two letters. One letter was from the Viet Cong and listed the conditions for Hertz's release. First a meeting was to be held on 8 February, four days before the letter arrived. In the same envelope was a second letter signed by her husband. It told of his good health and the hope that he would soon be freed.

Mrs. Hertz started knocking on doors for help. She appealed to the U.S. State Department, the CIA, the Vietnamese Catholic Church, and to France for intercession, but no one knew what to do about Gustav. Her troubles mounted. As the U.S. buildup continued, dependents were ordered out of the country. Nellie Hertz with her five children were repatriated to Leesburg, Virginia.

Back in Saigon, the war heated up. On 30 March 1965, Viet Cong terrorists bombed the U.S. Embassy, killing two Americans and twenty Vietnamese. Terrorist Nguyen Van Hai was wounded by shots fired by the Vietnamese police seconds before the blast. He fired back, killing a policeman, but was overpowered and taken into custody. A speedy trial followed and Hai was sentenced to be executed.

Radio Hanoi quickly broadcast an ultimatum: execute Hai and Hertz would die… a dilemma for both South Vietnam and the United States. The bombing had killed many innocent Vietnamese civilians whose relatives were demanding justice. The U.S. wanted Hertz alive and thus, Hai's execution was postponed. The situation was a standoff.

In the United States Mrs. Hertz again pounded on doors for help. Senator Robert Kennedy petitioned the representative of the Viet Cong's National Liberation Front stationed in Algiers, who replied that they would exchange Hertz for Hai. Kennedy sent the proposal to the State Department where it was stonewalled, "No Deal." The reasoning went, "If we trade a terrorist for a hostage now, what's going to prevent a new hostage from being taken each time a terrorist is caught?"

The matter was so politically volatile in South Vietnam that Washington feared the Vietnamese government might fall if Hai were released.

Months passed. The Hertz family did not give up. Crane Hertz, Gustav's son, met with the new ambassador from South Vietnam to the U.S., Vu Van Thai, and proposed the swap to him. He forwarded the inquiry to South Vietnam's Prime Minister Nguyen Cao Ky who agreed to the trade. Vietnamese hatred of Hai was cooling off. The State Department backpedaled, did a pirouette, and now accepted the Viet Cong proposal, which it had previously declined. It was Christmas 1965. By mid-January the Viet Cong replied that they were no longer interested in the swap. Another standoff.

A month later a ransom- note was received in Saigon. It claimed the Viet Cong would free Hertz for $20,000. The U.S. agreed and paid a VC agent, who promptly took the money and vanished without a trace. Hertz was not freed.

Meanwhile, VC Terrorist Nguyen Van Hai was cooling his heels in prison on Con Son Island. It was sheer coincidence that while all of this was taking place, I was assigned to establish and command a LORAN (Long Range Aid to Navigation) station on the island of Con Son. Little did I realize at the time that the assignment would thrust me into the middle of a game of international intrigue that had nothing to do with our mission of providing navigational assistance to U.S. Air and Sea forces in the theater of operation. My assignment had all the prospects of being routine and uneventful had it not been for the Hertz incident that occurred in Saigon shortly before my arrival.

Con Son island first developed by the French in 1892 as a penal colony, is the largest of a group of 14 islands located about 45 miles off the southern coast of Vietnam - a lush tropical paradise relatively safe from the intrusions of war on the mainland. Con Son served as a prison for South Vietnam as it did for France in the 19th and early 20th century. Many of the leaders of North Vietnam served time in Con Son prison when the French rules the country. Most notable among them was Ton Duc Thang who in 1969 succeeded Ho Chi Minh as the President of the Democratic Republic of Vietnam (North Vietnam).

Because of its French origin Con Son was sometimes called the second Devil's Island. It was home to over 4,500 people of whom 450 were soldiers of the South Vietnam Regional Forces assigned to defend the island and secure the prison. Two hundred South Vietnamese civil servants performed administrative duties. The prison population totaled 4,000; 2,500 of these were classified as political prisoners. The remaining 1,500 were every day criminals. Political prisoners were not just those who disagreed with the government. They included Vietnamese soldiers guilty of desertion or draft evasion.

So, when Nguyen Van Hai arrived on Con Son he received dual classification as both a political prisoner and a criminal. He was considered the most dangerous—and the most celebrated—of the 4,000 inmates. Each prisoner was assigned a security status and given work accordingly. Prison trustees lived in pairs in isolated coves around the island and reported by telephone any unusual sightings. Needless to say, this lookout duty was most desired.

But other jobs were also wanted. Work in the shops appealed to many. The brick factory, the mechanics shop, and the wood mill employed only the "better" prisoners. Work in the fields was also prized as an alternative to confinement. Even road repair work was sought after. Most of the prisoners remained locked up in five huge jail buildings. Each contained many cells about 20 feet wide by 30 feet long, where 70 to 80 inmates were held in cramped quarters.

Floors were concrete. Straw mats were the only comfort between the cement and a sleeping prisoner. In such a cell were kept 50 of the hardcore Viet Cong. Con Son was not a prisoner-of-war stockade, but a jail to house only the ringleaders, troublemakers, and other "special problems." Nguyen Van Hai was issued a straw mat and then he settled into life in the VC cell.

Rounding out the accommodations at Con Son were punishment cells of two types, "dark cells" and "tiger cages." The dark cells were solitary confinement areas measuring four feet by five feet. Prisoners were shackled to stone slabs, which were about four feet above the floor. When the door was closed the cell was totally dark. Con Son had ten of these for 4,000 prisoners. By comparison Alcatraz had six dark cells for 300 prisoners. However, at Alcatraz the cells were about eight feet square and there were no shackles. The tiger cages (pits dug into the ground) on Con Son were punishment cells for the unruly. It was possible to be put in the cage for a simple infraction of the rules, including refusing to salute either the flag of the U.S. or South Vietnam. All together there were 80 pit cells with bars on top and no windows. Each was five feet by nine feet and held three to five prisoners.

Con Son prison received most of its funding from the Agency for International Development (USAID). It is ironic that the U.S. tax dollars that had been buying food for Gustav Hertz before he was taken hostage were now buying fish, rice, and vegetables for VC terrorist Nguyen Van Hai. It was here on the island not far from the prison that we constructed the Loran Station.

Operation Tight Reign was the code name given to a classified undertaking to bring Loran C coverage to Southeast Asia. Ships or aircraft with the appropriate electronic equipment could measure the time difference in reception signals from transmitting stations, consult a calibrated map, and determine their position with 1/4 mile. The Coast Guard had a monopoly on Loran at that time so, when the U.S. Air Force wanted it in 1965, the Coast Guard got a green light to proceed with station construction. The locations of the components of the Southeast Asia Section were Sattahip, Thailand, Lampang, Thailand, Con Son, Republic of Vietnam, and Udorn,

Thailand. Operating crews were flown in from the United States to Bangkok while construction was still in progress and fanned out from Bangkok to their permanent stations to set about assisting with the construction. Living conditions were primitive. Tents were used for living quarters in most places and native food was sometimes all that was available. Communications, including mail service, were undependable. Transportation was irregular and hazardous. Supply routes varied with nearly every shipment.

Most travel to and from the Con Son station was by air. Commander Naval Support Activity Saigon scheduled twice-weekly flights from Saigon using C-47s. The U.S. Air Force flew C-123s into Con Son twice weekly. Prisoners came and went by boat with about 300 new ones arriving and about 300 old ones released every two months. The administration of the prison was liberal in that conjugal visits were permitted; families of deserving prisoners arrived once a month on Vietnamese Navy boats, and allowed to remain overnight.

When the Tight Reign construction party first arrived on Con Son, all the drinking water was flown in and those not preferring the salt-water beaches did bathing in a buffalo pond. The Loran station construction took place on the north end of the island separated from the village by a high mountain range. Along this mountainside a narrow, winding rough-surface, but all-weather road joined the village with the airstrip located at the north end close to the Loran site and other U.S. forces. In the village lived the Vietnamese Province Chief, Major Nguyen Van Ve and his Second-in-Command, Captain Tran.

In these early days a detachment of Special Forces had decided that they had made a mistake in trying to set up a training camp on Con Son and were pulling out the last of their material and personnel. Captain Deacon, the detachment commander who closed up the place, told me of some of the trails on the island. He recommended actions to take in the event of various hostile moves against the station. Then he boldly asserted that he could take the Loran Station with three men, a comment that stayed with me throughout the rest of my tour of duty.

On 2 September 1966, the flags were run up the pole and the station was placed in commission. Construction of the buildings by U.S. civilians was still going on. The crew no longer lived in tents even though the barracks was not finished. Dormitory style sleeping in the recreation room of the subsistence building had been ordered after two crewmen came down with falciparum malaria within one week.

Some of the prisoners were hired by the RMK-BRJ combine to assist with construction. They were paid 100 piasters per day (about $1.25 at the business exchange rate). They supplemented their food ration by catching rats, skinning them, and then roasting them on an improvised spit over an open fire.

Other U.S. forces were present on Con Son. The Navy operated a radar site while the army operated a Decca navigation station. The Loran station supported these units with fresh water, mail service, mess, Post Exchange, movies, and maintenance services.

In addition to commanding the Loran Station, I was also Senior Office Present of U.S. Forces. That meant that I had to keep a watchful eye on all U.S. activities on Con Son. The Red Cross paid routine visits to the prison for humanitarian purposes. Before they were due to arrive to inspect the treatment of the 50 Viet Cong, a lawyer from Military Assistance Command Vietnam (MACV) came to the island for a preliminary look-see. I accompanied him and Captain Tran into the large cell of Viet Cong. The VC were in good health and appeared content. The lawyer spoke with Captain Tran about the prisoners and then the inspection party left the cell. For about ten minutes I unknowingly shared a cell with my future adversary, terrorist Nguyen Van Hai.

Several prisoners were hired to help out around the Loran station. The officers and chiefs hired one as a houseboy. His duties included doing the laundry. Unfortunately, there was a language barrier and he couldn't tell the difference between the drum of soap powder, which was usually in the laundry room, and a large drum of powdered bleach, which he found there one day. The result was a strange-looking pile of clothes when he finished. But it didn't matter much because the clothes quickly wore out and were thrown away.

It was also his job to take a pressurized can of insect spray and use it around the quarters daily. One day he unwittingly got hold of a pressurized can of aluminum paint. Only a small amount got on the furniture but there were a number of glitzy bugs flying around Con Son for a while.

Recreational pastimes for the crew were many and varied. Movies were shown every night. A billiard table and pin pong table were set up in the day room. Magazines arrived regularly. Many books were on hand. Checkers, chess, and other games were plentiful. A stereo set, stereo tape recorders and recreational radio receivers were on hand. The service newspaper "Stars and Stripes" arrived with each mail delivery. A tennis court, volleyball court, badminton court and basketball court were built at the station. Fishing and hunting were popular and the beaches were splendid.

The Loran station filled a real need in Southeast Asia. Accurate aircraft navigation was a serious problem due to the remote location of many supply points, the mountainous terrain, and poor weather. The disruption of the Loran system would be a feather in the cap of any Viet Cong. In the cell of the hard-core VC in Con Son prison Nguyen Van Hai and his comrades were scheming away.

During the early morning darkness of 13 October 1966 the 50 imprisoned North Vietnamese made their move. In their 20-foot-high cell they formed a human ladder so that three of their number could escape through a hole ripped out of the roof. Nguyen Van Hai had no plastic explosives to use against the Loran Station Tower but he did not despair. He knew he was receiving special treatment. His execution had been delayed time and again. He had nothing to lose. He expected his charmed life to continue no matter what happened. Destroying the Loran Station would be a feather in his cap.

Pham Van Dau, another hard-core VC terrorist, was a veteran merchant of death. He had broken into a residence in Saigon and killed one American and two Vietnamese. He strangled them while they slept. Such skill and daring would prove invaluable in a foray against the Coast Guard station.

Le Hong Tu was the third escapee. He was probably chosen for his benign appearance. Whereas Hai and Dau looked mean and vicious, Tu was moon-faced and gregarious. He would be useful in communicating with others.

Food and drink would be needed for the seven-mile trip across the island so Tu was sent on a foraging expedition in Con Son village. It was daylight now and the Regional Forces were out hunting the escaped prisoners. They quickly found Tu and he was returned to custody.

When Tu failed to return, Hai and Dau decided to strike out by themselves. Some plants were edible and there might be coconuts along the trail that would furnish both food and drink. Rainwater could be found in rock crevices. Plus they had a little rice, which they had saved in jail from the daily rations and hidden from the guards. Major Ve, the Province Chief, was working up a lather. Hai was considered to be in his protective custody rather than an ordinary prisoner. Now he was neither. An interrogation of Tu revealed that the two VC were headed for the Loran station. How could Ve prevent some American from shooting Hai? He decided not to tell the U.S. Forces about the escape.

Major Ve assigned his deputy, Captain Tran, to head up the hunt for Hai and Dau. The island's size is about the same as New York City's Manhattan, but Con Son is a jungle not a metropolis. Most of the 450 Regional Forces already had duties to perform. But a company of 100 soldiers could be deployed. The most likely avenues that the escapees would follow would be either the 4-mile foot trail through the mountains or the desolate road winding 7 miles from the prison to the Loran site. Tran opted for the trail and stationed his troops in the jungle.

Meanwhile, the daily routine continued at the encampments of the U.S. Forces. Army, Navy, and Coast Guard personnel went about their indoor and outdoor duties unaware of the threat. The few civilians remaining from the construction company continued to live in tents on the Loran station. They thought their worst enemy was mosquitoes carrying malaria.

Captain Tran posted two soldiers as lookouts on a straight stretch of road near the Loran station just in case the VC were able to avoid contact with the RVN troops stationed in the Jungle. Soon they sighted the escapees crossing the road about a half a mile away. The Americans would have to be told he concluded. Any U.S. casualties would bring an investigation and unwanted publicity.

Five days after the escape Captain Tran sent word to Bruce Larrick, Project Superintendent of the civilian construction group, that the prisoners were loose. Larrick, to his great credit, immediately informed me and I alerted all U.S. Forces on the island. There was a chorus of clicks as door locks snapped shut. Defensive positions were set in place at the Loran station. Side arms were issued to the officers and chief petty officers—Colt 45s to be worn at all times. The crew's weapons were aged M-1 rifles—the only ones in Vietnam and were issued to watch standers. The roving security watch was linked to the operations watch via radio. Operations were coordinated by phone through the station. Off-duty personnel were ordered to remain inside. Necessary trips outside would be made in pairs.

A show of force was made during daylight hours by parking a pickup truck at the main entrance to the fenceless station. Two crewmen with M-1s were posted in the truck. The picture windows in the prefab operations building were blacked out with shower curtains. All doors and windows remained locked 24 hours a day. A lock was hurriedly installed on the shack containing the garbage in realization that hungry men would eat anything in order to survive.

I was aware of the dangers present from the nature of the construction of the subsistence building. The total ceiling was made of drop paneling. Panels could be lifted; then locked spaces could be entered from above including the armory and—ten feet away—my quarters. Needless to say I slept with my 45 loaded and placed under my bed.

A Vietnamese sound truck drove up and down the road alongside the station calling for the surrender of the escapees. Fully armed Vietnamese soldiers roamed the adjacent hills. Time was running out for the VC. Their food and water were gone with no more to be had.

On 19 October Dau surrendered and two days later the stubborn and tenacious Nguyen Van Hai was flushed from hiding less than 50 yards from the main entrance to the Loran station. Major Ve said that the escapees would be given military trials and probably executed. Six weeks later he told me that Nguyen Van Hai had died of "stomach trouble." It was 5 December 1966. His "stomach trouble" began at the time of the Embassy bombing when a policeman shot him in the stomach.

With 300 prisoners being released and returned to the mainland every two months, it was not long before the Viet Cong learned of Hai's fate through the grapevine. On 15 June 1967 a Viet Cong broadcast implied that Gustav Hertz had been executed in reprisal.

The U.S. responded by cooperating on a LIFE Magazine cover story of 21 July 1967 that carried a picture of Hai with the caption, "Hai is alive today, in a South Vietnamese prison." In the body of the story appeared, "Hai, the man whose fate was interlinked with that of Hertz, is still alive in a prison outside Saigon." It was doubtlessly the best information that the U.S. diplomats possessed. But the Viet Cong were unconvinced. They knew that Hai had been held on Con Son—not outside Saigon. And the photo in Lirh was taken right after the bombing of the U.S. Embassy. The U. S. did not possess recent photos of Hai—not even the mug shot of Hai taken on Con Son.

Truth is sometimes elusive in the world of diplomacy. The Viet Cong reaction to the LIFE article was to resurrect Gustav Hertz with two letters—the first from the chairman of the National Liberation Front, Nguyen Huu Tho, to Cambodia's chief of state, Prince Norodam Sihanouk, and the second letter from Sihanouk to Nellie Hertz. The VC allowed Hertz to "live" three more months, and then it was announced that he died of malaria on 24 September. "Stomach trouble" claimed Hai. "Malaria" took Hertz. It was the final standoff.

Each of two key people involved in this drama was acting conscientiously in what each believed was the best interest of his country. There were heroes and villains. But a big hero to one group was a big villain to another. With the passage of time the distinction between heroes and villains becomes blurry. Eventually, there are only the living and the dead.

ABOUT THE AUTHOR: Ralph W. Judd commanded the LORAN station on Con Son Island from August 1966 to July 1967. He resides in San Francisco, California.

SURVIVORS
By Michael Young

I heard the unmistakable hiss of the first rocket-propelled grenade even before I saw it. I knew from experience the B-40 (a point detonating, shoulder launched anti-tank weapon) was effective and deadly. As I studied its rapid approach, I realized it was aimed directly at the port side of our patrol boat (PBR). I watched almost dispassionately as it augured the fiberglass, passing through the bow with a hollow thunk-thunk as it punched a neat hole in the port side and immediately exited the starboard to detonate against a tree. Certain it had been launched from a point about eighty yards away on the river's north bank, I trained my M-16 assault rifle on that position only to see a second B-40 had been fired. I stood on the port engine hatch beside the M-60 machine gunner and frantically emptied the magazine of my rifle. As expended cartridges pinged off my helmet, I watched the second rocket zig and turn straight for me.

"Oh shit," I said, then watched in utter amazement as the B-40 dipped at the very last instant to penetrate the hull directly beneath me. Its impact bounced me six inches off the hatch.

I was aware the round had not exploded normally, and was extremely grateful it hadn't. I slammed another magazine into my M-16 and resumed firing, deafened by the cacophony of sound generated by the formidable weapons of two PBRs, all of which were firing at once. Our boats headed downriver in an attempt to flee the ambush zone, but mine began to slow, sinking. I leaned over the side, hanging on for dear life to the M-60 machine gun mount. My heart was pounding as I noted the football-size hole right at the water line.

On the Vam Co Tay River that morning in 1969, as a passenger in transit, I was under orders to relocate within the River Patrol Force and anxious to get to Saigon for several promised days of rest. I was not at all anxious to be involved in another firefight. Since my in-country transfers had so far been many and frequent, I had no real sense of permanence, no base I could call home. As a result, I'd seen action in much of the southern fourth of South Vietnam. Tired to the point of exhaustion from constant involvement in what I angrily called "an exercise in too much sacrifice for too little return," I'd long been asking myself, "What the hell are we doing here?"

I caught my breath and turned to the Chief Gunners Mate, then placed my hand on his shoulder and squeezed. Trying hard to override the awesome bark of the forward fifty caliber machine guns and the M-60 pounding to my immediate left, I hollered, "Chief! We're sinking, goddammit! Beach! Beach the boat!"

I backed up the verbal warning with a signal — hand outstretched, flat, palm down, all fingers pointing towards the shore — just to be sure the man got the message. Then I reached past him, scooped up the microphone attached to the boat's radio and yelled into it. "Lansing Delta One to Delta Two, over!"

The companion PBR immediately answered, "Delta Two aye! Go!"

"Delta Two, we're gonna beach! When we do, cover our collective asses! Do you copy?" I watched Delta Two accelerate and close to within several hundred feet, but couldn't hear the other boat's response through the chaos of weapons firing, roaring engines, screamed obscenities, and the relentless noise of my own inner confusion.

Seconds later, Delta One beached in a wild cascade of spray and mud, finally coming to rest with ten feet of stern still in the water. We had run aground with all weapons firing, for we had no idea what might have been waiting in the heavy jungle foliage. I watched in awe as the forward fifty caliber machine guns completely chopped through a small stand of trees.

The chief screamed, "Cease fire! Cease fire!" The overwhelming thunder of weaponry trailed off into sporadic rifle fire until it finally died out altogether. After I confirmed the undamaged Delta Two had taken up an oval pattern to the rear of our boat as protection from any threats lurking on the opposite river bank, I immediately called

Lansing, the small U.S. Naval base to which the two boats were assigned.

The radio operators at Lansing, located some ten kilometers away, were quick to respond. "Delta One, we copied your transmissions. We know you got trouble. Advise."

"Roger Lansing," I answered. "Wait. Delta One out."

A battery of worried eyes were focused on me, for I was the ranking officer on scene. Although not officially in command, and having already decided that whatever lay under the left engine hatch had become our most pressing problem, I turned to the chief, the actual patrol officer, and asked, "Know anything about B-40's that don't blow?"

He shook his head. "No sir, not a damn thing."

"Well, neither do I." I took a moment to pull my thoughts together. "Chief, this is your show. You're the man in charge here and I'm not gonna pull rank. I'll work with you, take over, whatever you want. It's up to you."

The chief was a man of average height, build, and intelligence who had served with the Navy for some fifteen years. A lifer quite familiar with protocol, and a volunteer for duty in Vietnam, he clearly understood that his courage and ability were not in question. He said, "I got no problem handin' this off, sir. Maybe you'll see somethin' I'd miss. I'll help any way I can." He stepped back to stand among the crew.

I decided several unpleasant options were open: the PBR Could be abandoned on shore, or towed into the river and sunk. The least attractive, removal of the B-40, had been the first to enter my mind, but I found myself resisting it. So I radioed Lansing, summarized the situation and asked to speak to someone familiar with enemy ordinance.

"Delta One," Lansing responded, "we got UDT (Under Water Demolition Team) people here in the shack with us."

I grinned. I'd worked with enough Underwater Demolition Teams to know a few members of UDT at times seemed to border on the insane. But I also knew they were awfully good at what they did.

"Okay Lansing, put your man on the horn."

The radio fairly crackled with the voice. "Delta One, there ain't no way to disarm a B-40. No way. It's too simple, just made to go 'bang' on impact. We advise you give it the once over, then let us know its condition. We'll tell you what we think based on what you see."

There was a pause, then came a different voice. "Lansing Delta One, Lansing is standing by."

I figured they had more chiefs than Indians.

I swallowed hard, then gingerly lifted the engine hatch to find a damaged B-40 lying on a hot diesel engine. With the microphone in one hand, cord stretched taut, I transmitted a description.

"Lansing, the thing looks like an exploded cone, and it's about the size of a grapefruit — maybe a little bigger. It's split wide-open, guts exposed, and its nose is torn apart. There's something that looks like gunpowder packed around a twisted metal core, which looks intact, but appears to be oozing white phosphorous. Shrapnel's spread all over the engine." I stepped back from the compartment and released the microphone button.

The ensuing radio silence was finally punctured by the second UDT voice. "Delta One, we think your little item can still explode, especially if you're rough with it. We suggest you remove it to the river. Submerge it. We advise extreme caution."

I laughed. I considered the warning unnecessary. After a final, "Delta One, confirm your intentions," UDT suspended transmission.

Only the chief and I were on board, for during the various radio exchanges the crew had gone ashore. As the others departed, I'd overheard one crew member say, "They tell us never to get off the friggin' boat, 'cause the bush is so much worse. Right now, the bush looks awful damn good to me."

It looked good to me, too. I was sweating profusely as I paced back and forth. After several moments of tense deliberation, I grabbed the microphone and said coldly, "Lansing, this is Delta One. I'm gonna do it... Will advise."

I bent down to lean over the compartment opening, then extended my right hand and gently grasped the remnants of the B-40. I lifted it away from the engine, then up and out of the compartment. I felt myself starting to shake, but concentrated on remaining calm. I figured UDT had suggested river immersion for reasons other than the obvious. I was pretty sure they were counting on the water to absorb some of the explosive force, if the B-40 even decided to blow. I drew small comfort from that as I carefully made my way aft; holding the device away and to my front so I could keep it level and see where I was going.

I crouched at the stern and steadied myself with my left hand. Sweat coursed into both eyes, stinging and clouding my vision, but I dared not wipe my brow. As I felt the B-40 getting heavier, I decided it was damn well time to end the exercise, so I very gently lowered the device into the water. I released my grip the moment it was totally submerged, then backed away and watched it sink. It did not explode.

The chief waited a moment or two, then headed aft. As he brushed past, I said under my breath, "I almost wish that son-of-a-bitch had blown up." He gave me an odd look, but said nothing as he opened a storage hatch, brought out a life vest, inserted it into the hole at the waterline and pulled the inflation cord. After a short wait, during which all hands seemed to be expecting a delayed detonation, the others filed silently on board. Delta Two then dragged our disabled Delta One from shore and we both got underway at one half normal speed.

"Lansing, this is Delta One. The B-40's in the river. Two boats are enroute with an E.T.A. of four-zero minutes. We have no casualties. Delta One out." As I slid my thumb off the microphone button, I let it snap to with an audible "pop."

Lansing acknowledged at once. "Roger, Delta One. Lansing out."

Angry for reasons I didn't yet clearly understand, I took a seat aft as the shakes returned. I offered up silent thanks when the radio finally went totally mute.

I studied the eddies stirred up around the life jacket protruding from Delta One's port side like some grotesque, unwanted growth, then gradually shifted my gaze to the mesmerizing white foam churned up by the lead PBR, laboring hard under the additional load. When an incessant popping suddenly burst into my awareness, I realized the drone of Delta Two's engines had almost completely numbed my senses. I studied the hovering Seawolf helicopter and felt sure the whup-whup of its blades would forever remind me of Vietnam.

Upon our return to Lansing the M-60 machine gunner whispered, "Damn good job, lieutenant, damn good." No one else ever said a word.

That evening, sequestered in the relative security of the Meyerkord Hotel in Saigon, I had time to do a little thinking. So I wrote my girl a letter in which I detailed the incident, replete with my every thought and feeling. I wrote fast, concerned about nothing other than getting thought onto paper.

When finished, I read what I'd written. 1s I read, several paragraphs seemed to leap from the page. They went something like this.

"I took a big risk today, which I was willing to do, in part because I felt I owed those men, and simply because it's my job. But I can't understand why I feel it was futile, just another in an endless string of meaningless deeds in a war that seems to have no meaning. None whatsoever.

I wonder how many other deeds, so many with deadly consequence, are daily performed unceremoniously in this God-forsaken place. Girl, I'm where death, or the risk of it, is simply something to be tolerated until the lucky survivors can go home. But home is nothing more than a place where no one cares, or wants to hear, what we've done."

I was shaken by my own words, but I read on.

"I've begun to seriously question whether survivors have all the luck in the deadly game we play here — the game of war in which it seems those who die are chosen by the whimsy of some cosmic crap shoot whose outcome doesn't seem to matter. For the rest of our lives we survivors will have to carry the memory of what we did — both the good and the bad — and the hard knowledge that the only lesson of war is that we've long ago outgrown any need for the lesson."

I had read enough. I angrily folded the page, then held the small packet of paper between both hands and tore it up. I ripped each piece into ever smaller pieces until only confetti remained. I shaped my hands like a pair of little plows, carefully formed the confetti into a small pile on the desktop and shoveled it off, hard, onto the floor. I crushed the shards underfoot.

I'd decided nothing was going to stop me from getting roaring, flaming drunk. Intent on finding some nondescript dive on Tu Do Street, I strapped on a sidearm, left the room, then resolutely made my way to the dark and garbage-filled street below.

ABOUT THE AUTHOR: Michael (Mike) Young served with the River Patrol Flotilla 5 from November 1968 to March 1969. He resides in Winder, Georgia.

THE GENERAL'S LATRINE

By Lieutenant Colonel Robert W. Michel, U.S. Army Retired

Some say that the portable latrine system first introduced by the military in Vietnam was the forerunner of the present day "Don's John" and "Port O Potties". The system resembled the age-old outhouse, with a catch basin cut from 55 gallon fuel barrels. The latrine enclosures were easily moved by forklift and could be clustered in groups or singularly placed in a convenient, downwind, location. The innovation put an end forever to the time consuming and dirty job of digging a sanitary trench. In 1966, a tale about one of those latrines made the rounds in Vietnam. The story was too vivid in detail to have been contrived.

In the mid-1960s, reacting to the build up of American forces in Vietnam, the military chose to construct a major facility to house the vast number of logistical and administrative personnel that were flooding the country. A site was chosen 20 miles north of Saigon near the town of Long Binh. Saigon, at the time, was overcrowded with US troops from every branch of the service, many of whom were destined to be relocated to Long Binh. The installation, which grew rapidly in size, consisted of row upon row of hastily constructed wooden buildings similar to the structures built on military installations in the US during World War II, except that they lacked plumbing of any kind. Personal sanitation was taken care of using portable showers and latrines scattered strategically throughout the installation.

It seems that on the occasion of the relocation of a Military Police Brigade from Saigon to Long Binh, the Brigade Commander, a gruff, no nonsense Brigadier General, insisted that the relocation be carried out with the utmost speed and efficiency-"There would be no wasted motion", he was heard to say.

On the day of arrival at Long Binh, the Brigade Headquarters was bustling with activity. Desks were moved into place, telephones were installed and the administrative staff was busy getting organized. The General, who was surveying the operation turned, at one point to his aide-de-camp, a lieutenant, and asked, "Where are the latrines?"

"Let me show you, sir." the aide answered and ushered the General to a row of windows in the building. "See those six latrines on the hill over there?" pointing out of the window. "They've been assigned to us."

"That's unacceptable," replied the General. "Much too inconvenient. Our people will waste far too much time running back and forth to the latrine. Call the installation engineer's office and have them send someone to move the latrines over to there..." pointing out the window to a spot closer to the headquarters building.

A few hours later, a young soldier wearing the stripes of Private First Class (PFC), who looked as though he was fresh out of high school, appeared in front of the aide's desk and announced that he was sent to move the latrines.

"Come with me" the aide said, taking the soldier by the arm to one of the windows. "See those latrines over there on the hill?"

"Yes, sir." answered the soldier.

"Move them down closer to the headquarters." pointing to the General's preferred location. The soldier snapped a salute, left the building and climbed aboard his forklift.

A few minutes had passed when someone was heard to shout, "Where's the General?"

"Who wants to know?" a voice hollered back.

"MACV Headquarters is on the phone and wants to talk to him" came the reply.

Another voice piped in, "I think he went to the latrine."

A hush fell over the headquarters staff as they all raced to the windows to view the progress of the forklift. The vehicle was about 20 feet from the latrines when someone in the building said, "Surely he has enough sense to knock on the door before moving the latrine."

Not this soldier. As he maneuvered his forklift behind the first latrine, the General's aide ran in panic out onto the porch of the building, cupped his hand around his mouth and shouted, "Stop! Stop!" but it was to no avail. The engine noise of the forklift drowned out his plea.

The driver jockeyed the forklift into position; swiftly raised the latrine four feet into the air and without hesitation started down the hill toward the headquarters building.

Abruptly, the door of the latrine flew open to reveal the General framed in the doorway, his fatigue pants around his ankles and a look of disbelief on his face. He braced himself with his arms against the rocking motion of the latrine as the forklift bounced its way over the rough terrain. Then, with one hand holding the doorframe for stability, he reached with his other to pull up his pants and, in the process, almost lost his balance. Some of the on-lookers in the headquarters gasped in horror as he tried to regain his composure and avoid falling forward under the wheels of the forklift. When finally his pants were in place, the General swung himself out of the door onto the ground, signaling with outstretched arms for the driver to stop and dismount the forklift.

What happened next brought chuckles from the headquarters staff. The fork lift driver now at rigid attention and obviously petrified, was being lectured forcefully by the General whose indignation was evident by the abrupt movement of his arms as he vehemently made his point. The soldier, on the other hand, probably had never seen a General before and undoubtedly expected to face a firing squad in the morning. His face was ashen and he shook uncontrollably.

When the General finished with the hapless GI and turned to walk to the headquarters building, staff members scurried to their desks to await the aftermath of the "Old Man's" rage. When the screen door to the building slammed shut, announcing his arrival, everyone jumped to their feet and stood silent and stone faced as he entered the room. The General gazed grimly at each person through squinted eyes. You could hear a pin drop. Then, slowly, his expression changed to a smile followed by a hearty belly laugh that instantly took the chill out of the air. Everyone broke into hysterical laughter. The "Old Man" had a sense of humor after all.

ABOUT THE AUTHOR: See "Rainbow Charlie".

THE CAVE

By Commander Paul L. Bennett, U.S.N. Retired

Back in 1965 in Vietnam, surveillance missions were frequently conducted in L-19 aircraft, "Bird Dogs" as they were known, a single prop plane about the size and configuration of the familiar Piper Cub. The Junk Force Advisors periodically would fly backseat to get a look at their entire patrol area. The idea was to patrol the coast looking for boats entering or leaving the many tributaries along the shoreline. The plane's top speed was approximately 87 knots or about 100 miles per hour; however, so many modifications had been made increasing the weight of the plane that most of the Bird Dogs had difficulty making 70 knots.

The pilots were Ensigns or Junior Grades (JG's) fresh out of flight school and seemed to possess two common characteristics: over sized gonads and insanity. They loved to take up new Advisors and make them barf as well as scare the living shit out of them by doing stalls and loops or dropping down so low that the tree branches were above the wings. Of course, Bird Dogs were never intended to be warplanes. The only protection for the pilot and the spotter was the two or three flak jackets that they sat on. It usually worked out better if the advisor were a little crazy as well. The backseater would customarily bring his M-16 rifle, a dozen or so fragmentary grenades and sometimes propaganda leaflets.

A favorite weapon was an empty Coca Cola bottle inserted into a full roll of toilet paper. The sound made by the bottle as it descended was incredibly similar to that of a full-fledged 500-pound bomb. Advisors were known to buzz American patrol boats, free fire zones or even their own bases just for the hell of it.

Another interesting toy for the backseater was a long handle strapped to the left firewall. Next to the handle were complete instructions on how to remove it, insert it between one's legs into a slotted receptacle on the floor and then fly the plane from the backseat! You did this, of course, only after the pilot had been killed. Presumably, the backseater, who may or may not have any flying experience, would be able to land the plane safely by some form of osmosis. The rumor mill had it that an advisor in the Delta had actually accomplished this little trick and lived to tell about it, but the story was never verified to anyone's satisfaction.

The pilots had also modified the planes by jury-rigging a cluster of 2.75 inch rockets onto each wing. Each cluster held four rockets that could be released by the pilot by jerking hard on an attached wire. If the rockets were let go one wing at a time, it would put a severe twist on the plane that was hard to control. If the rockets were released simultaneously, it slowed the plane down to stall speed. Since the wings were not designed for this kind of stress, it seemed only to be a matter of time before someone lost a wing - but it was one of those things that one didn't spend a lot of time thinking about.

"Let's get our asses out of here or we'll never get the zone covered," Sully said as he made the final adjustments to his seat cushions and flak jackets. Jeremiah Aloyisious Sullivan III was from Somerville, Massachusetts. He had graduated from Boston College where he majored in girls, parties and hockey, in that order. After five and a half years of college life he somehow amassed enough credits for his degree, so following in the footsteps of father and old brother, he joined the Navy. There was a lingering rumor at BC that it was the Dean of Students himself who prevailed upon several of Sully's professors to expedite his matriculation. He felt that he could no longer devote such an inordinate amount of time to dealing with Sully's various adventures considering that he had several thousand other students who also needed his attention.

The Navy, particularly in 1964, was in desperate need of pilots so Sully's lengthy and unimpressive transcript was given only token scrutiny, and he was in Pensacola in short order. Once free of the party distraction that had taken up the majority of his time and energies over the past several years, Sully did a fair job in his academics and exceptionally well in the air. He had heard that the rulebook had not quite caught up with the war in Vietnam so he volunteered and was in country within a month of getting his wings. Lieutenant Junior Grade (LTJG) Bob Boyer, Junk Force Advisor from the Island of Binh Ba off the coast of Cam Ranh Bay, was Sully's backseat.

"I hope to hell we see something today, Sully. This war is getting boring." Both officers had been in Vietnam for about four months. While Sully spent his time in the air nearly every day, Boyer flew only two or three times a month. There were six advisors in the Nha Trang Coastal Zone and they took turns coming into Nha Trang to fly with Sully or one of the other Bird Dog pilots. Sully also had to give sightseeing tours whenever a REMF (Rear Echelon Mother Fucker) was in town from the States or Saigon and he detested doing it. The Coastal Surveillance Command (CSC) Commanding Officer had, on numerous occasions, warned Sully about his conduct and language when giving the VIP tour to visiting high roller civilian or military guests. "All they're doin' is getting an hour ride so they can put themselves in for a fuckin' medal or get their pictures in the paper for being in combat. Nine times out of ten we don't see shit or even get shot at but to hear it from those assholes they just went through World War Three!"

Sully did the visual inspection of the Bird Dog, lit off the engine, checked with the CSC and Operations Control and then headed into the wind over the water. Since he and Boyer had flown together a dozen or so times, Sully didn't have to indoctrinate his backseat and they immediately headed north at about a thousand feet checking the coastal traffic.

"I'll take us up north over the mountain and then we can work the Islands coming back south", said Sully over the intercom.

"Roger that, Sul. How 'bout swingin' in close to the mountain" I want to get a picture of a real live 'free fire zone' for my memoirs."

"Can do, Bob."

The Vietnamese Province Chief had declared an area of several thousand acres directly north of Nha Trang a free fire zone. Anyone caught in the area was automatically assumed to be a Viet Cong and could be summarily shot on sight. Additionally, planes returning to either carriers or land bases could dump their unexpended bombs in any of the designated free fire zones.

Sully banked left and brought the Bird Dog to within a few hundred feet of the mountain. Boyer was focusing his camera when he spotted a figure along the face of the mountain emerging from the crevice adjoining what appeared to be a small cave.

"Sully, there's a guy on the cliff face. Black pajamas. Looks like an old man. Can you swing back?"

Sully once more maneuvered to make an approach on the mountain. This time he came in at an angle that would give a better visual of the cave. They saw the man at the same time. He was elderly with a white mane and wore the traditional black pajamas and Ho Chi Minh sandals. He was carrying a rifle and as they watched he calmly inserted a single bullet into it, jammed the bolt forward, aimed and damn near put that bullet through Sully's head as it tore through the plastic windshield two inches to the right of Sully's ear.

"Sonofabitch!" Sully screamed as he pulled violently on his controls to clear the side of the mountain. The old man scurried back towards the cave.

"Stand by for heavy rolls, Backseat. I'm going after that bastard!" Sully screamed through his intercom. Boyer got rid of his camera, grabbed his AR-15 and checked his supply of grenades.

"Can you believe that little prick? I'm gonna waste him!" Sully shouted.

He spun the small plane to the south and prepared his wire rope that would trip his rockets. He also called into operations at the CSC to report that he had received fire and was about to retaliate. The CSC acknowledged the report and asked for coordinates.

"Just how in hell am I supposed to fly this piece of junk, shoot back at the VC and figure out a location all at the same time?" he spit into the intercom and gave the CSC a 'Wait, Out'. Concentrating on the cave, he came in full throttle and used the only fire control system available - the Mark One Eyeball. He let go with both clusters and the damn Bird Dog almost stopped in midair. Boyer could feel his chest squeezing with the pressure. He whacked his head as the small plane bucked and Sully fought to regain control. Boyer strained to follow the flight of the rockets as they headed towards the cave. He watched as the port cluster hit high on the left wall of the entrance and the starboard cluster hit absolutely bull's-eye on the cave.

"Right on the money, Sully! You just cleaned his clock", Boyer yelled.

Sully swung the plane back out over the water and checked all of his instruments to assure himself that there was no damage.

"Well, at least we rattled his brains some. Let's swing by for one more look."

The Bird Dog was far more maneuverable now that it no longer carried the rocket clusters on its wings. Grayish smoke and dust lingered in the cave entrance as they approached. Out of the center of it strode the old man who once again slowly and carefully took a single round from his pocket, chambered the round, aimed carefully and shot. Boyer was on him immediately with automatic fire from his AR-15 kicking up dirt and rock all around him as the old man dove for cover.

"Well, I'll be damned," Sully signed through the intercom. "Jesus, I can't believe it," he said with genuine admiration.

"We don't have the time or ammo to muck around anymore with him but I'm not going to forget that old bastard for awhile. Let's get some good coordinates to the CSC for future reference.

Later in the day as we neared the end of our patrol we got a call from the Coastal Surveillance Center asking for our location and fuel report. We replied that we were in route to Nha Trang and had about an hour more of fuel. The CSC asked us for a target of opportunity for the cruiser CANBERRA which was positioned off the free fire zone where we had our encounter with the old man earlier in the day. "I sure as hell have a target," Sully said to Boyer over the intercom. "You aren't seriously going to sick that cruiser on that old guy are you?" Boyer asked. "You bet your ass I am?" Sully yelled. Sully repeated the coordinates to the CSC and shifted frequencies to speak directly to the ship whose call sign was 'Boomer'. "Boomer, Boomer, this is Shoo Fly Pie, how do you read me?" "Shoe Fly Pie, this is Boomer. Loud and clear. How me? Over." "Five by five, Boomer. Hear you want to get rid of some bullets."

"That's a Roger, Shoe Fly Pie. First day in country and we'd like Charley to know we've arrived."

"I'm getting low on gas but I'll get you started and be back to check battle damage in about a half hour," Sully said. "Give me five to get on station."

Sully positioned the Bird Dog north of the cave, rechecked the coordinates and called for a single eight inch round. Canberra responded within seconds and as tremendous explosion sounded from the mountain just north of the cave.

"Drop 200. Fire for affect," Sully directed.

Within five minutes and five more rounds Sully had the cruiser's guns right on the mouth of the cave. "Boomer, this is Shoe Fly Pie. You are right on. Continue firing. I'm headed to the gas station. Permission to depart?'

"Pergra, Shoe Fly, any friendly anywhere near my target?" Boomer responded.

"No Sir. It's all Indian Country. Fire at will," Sully replied.

In short order the Bird Dog had landed at Nha Trang and as the ground crew gassed and checked out the plan Sully and Boyer relieved themselves, ate an old cheese sandwich and a warm coke and prepared to take off again. "I ain't got time to fix that windshield, Sir. If it doesn't bother you too much I'll get it after this trip," the crew chief said to Sully.

"Don't sweat it, Chief. We should be back in an hour and you can catch it then" Sully said.

As soon as they were airborne again Sully was on the radio to Canberra. "Boomer, Boomer. This is Shoe Fly Pie. Will be at your location in 10. How goes it?"

"Roger, Shoe Fly. Have expended 75 five inch and 90 eight inch. Will cease fire at this time and wait for damage assessment," the cruiser reported.

"Holy Shit?" Boyer exclaimed. "That's ahelluva lot of taxpayer's money for one old man, Sully."

"Aw, we would have unloaded somewhere else if not there, so what the hell. At least we had a target," he said.

"Boomer, this is Shoe Fly. Please verify you have ceased fire, I'm going in for a look," Sully said.

The face of the mountain was now cratered and redesigned by the impacts of the shells. It was difficult to see where the cave had been and a dust cloud lingered above the whole area. Battle damage assessment (BDA) was a judgment call on the part of the spotter and it could be a crucial tool in jacking up or crashing crew morale. Sully saw a good opportunity to do some good for the ship and also be fairly accurate about his assessment. "Boomer, this is Shoe Fly. BDA follows: target destroyed. Possible VC battalion headquarters and ammo dump completely obliterated. Well Done, Boomer!" Sully and Boyer both could hear the background cheers of the crew on the ship as Boomer responded, "Shoe Fly, this is Boomer. Nice working with you. Hope to see you again soon."

"Roger that, Boomer. Nice shooting. Request permission to head to the barn?"

"Permission granted," the cruiser responded as it came about and continued north in search of more calls for fire.

Sully brought the Bird Dog in on a nice three-point landing and he and Boyer headed to the CSC to make their final report. Boyer's monthly trip to Nha Trang was coming to an end. He spent the next two days shopping for odds and ends that he would need to get him through the next several weeks on the Island. On his last night he hooked up with Sully and two other young aviators to get some chow at one of the local fly palaces. Eating in what was called a restaurant in Vietnam invariably became a two-handed exercise as one waved frantically at the flies while trying to stab food with chopsticks. Sometimes the effort burned more energy than the food provided but it was just another thing to get used to. One of the other pilots was a Texan who naturally answered to the nickname 'Tex'.

Tex had flown the coast during the day with another Junk Force Advisor as his backseat. "You know we had us a good time today," he said. "Mah backseat upchucked right in his own lap a minute after takeoff and had to live with that garbage for two hours. He was so pissed by the time we got back he didn't even say goodbye."

"Some asshole up on the mountain took a couple of pot shots at us and caught a wing. The backseat nearly shit his pants on top of his other problems," Tex chuckled.

Sully and I exchanged glances and said nearly simultaneously, "What the hell did he look like, Tex?"

"Oh, he was just some old man - white hair, black pajamas, Ho Chi Minh sandals - the usual," he said as he tried to separate the flies from his bowl of rice.

"Where exactly was he?" Boyer asked.

"Well, you remember where Boomer was blastin' the hell out of that free fire zone the other day? He was right in the middle of that area. If he was in a cave it must have been a mile deep the way that cruiser beat up on that mountain. Funny thing too was that his rifle must have been a hundred years old. The son of a bitch had to single load it, jack the slug home and then pop it off. It was almost like slow motion."

Sully just stared at Boyer. He was remembering a recent quote by President Johnson about how soon the boys would be coming home. He thought to himself that if the Viet Cong had a bunch of people running around with the balls of that old man, it was going to be one awful long war.

ABOUT THE AUTHOR: Paul Bennett served two tours in Vietnam. One tour as an advisor in 1965-66 and the other as Commanding Officer of the USS Crocket from November 1968 to January 1969. He resides in Princeton, Massachusetts with his wife Mary.

A CASE OF MISTAKEN IDENTITY
By David W. Schill

I was part of the Navy's construction forces, better known as the Seabees, based in Chu Lai south of Da Nanang. I was just getting used to life there, when I was told to pack my bags and move north to our farthest outlying detachment, Cua Viet.

My new duty station was located about as far north as one could go without setting foot in North Vietnam. It was situated on the coast of the China Sea at the mouth of the Song Cua Viet River. The installation was but a football field in size and housed a joint force made up of men from the U.S. Navy, U.S. Army and Vietnamese Navy. The sailors from both Navies conducted river operation while the U.S. Army provided security. It was a diverse group indeed.

Cua Viet is probably familiar to Marines who served in Northern Quang Tn Province prior to 1970. Some considered it a rest area, but in my view, it was starkly different from Chu Lai. It was not a command center where generals and admirals ran around issuing orders and receiving reports. It was a very small dot on a map full of much larger dots. The compound was littered with debris, junk, shacks, communications antennae, power lines on utility poles, and sand, lots of sand.

Most of the buildings on the compound were single story living quarters or "hooch's" as they were known. A hooch contained about a dozen men, along with cots, plywood footlockers, metal stand-up lockers (if you were lucky enough to get your hands on one), and anything else you could obtain to provide creature comforts. Each resident of a hooch would typically have a cot, which he called his own, walled in with lockers or stacked footlockers. Primitive living to say the least, especially for a sailor.

My time was spent in the daily routine of military construction. I was initially assigned to one of the two cement mixers on the job site. We batched our own concrete and burned out several engines in the process, because of their continuous use. As time went on, I became a truck driver. Being a driver got me out of the sun and allowed me to ride around sitting down, which was a blessing.

Our trucks were used for supply runs or whatever else was required. "Pothole patrol" was one such task. It involved at least two dump trucks and a road grader, and required hauling road-fill from our camp to a bomb crater that had been identified as a hazard to our operation. Then we'd fill it. On one occasion I was chosen to be a driver on a pothole mission about five miles or so down the road from us. I hooked up a water trailer to my truck and picked up a load of dirt, grabbed my crew, and lined up with the other trucks at the ammunition resupply point to take on extra ammo. Anyone assigned to work outside the compound was required to be armed and have another person in the vehicle. It was reminiscent of the 'shotgun' guard in the stagecoach days. We were loaded for bear when our little convoy, in single file, departed for the day's adventure. My 'shotgun' and I were eating everyone's dust in last place.

When we arrived at our destination we filled the hole and then ran over it to provide some compaction. After we were done, we dragged our feet returning to base camp hoping to avoid being assigned another task. With the trucks riding empty it was common for us to have some fun. We would pair off, one truck against another in our version of a drag race. The man riding shotgun on the grader would stand between the trucks and give the "go" signal with the drop of his hand. Then each driver would pop the clutch and floor the gas pedal. The noise level was intense and the excitement great. Roaring monster trucks belching black diesel smoke and swirling reddish dust from their undercarriages. Once the lever was pulled in the cabin selecting the upper case gearbox, another five gears became available and the race was really on.

On this particular trip we had three vehicles full of drag racing enthusiasts and it was my turn to go against an opponent, so I lined up next to the grader. The flag was raised, engines gunned, smoke belched, fan belts squealed, and Seabees eyed each other with that 'I'm gonna blow your doors off' look. The flagman dropped his arm and the clutches popped. It was the ultimate 'pedal to metal' and I was determined to be the first to beat the mighty grader. I was just reaching down to the floor to grab the lever and transfer to the upper case gearbox when my eye caught the grader sliding by. I yanked the lever with all my might, bending it at an odd upward angle. My shotgun was shouting encouraging words and throwing things at the grader. I skipped first gear and went right into second and kept on shifting until I reached fifth gear and my trucks top speed of 35 miles per hour. I finally had to admit that the grader had beaten me, and to my surprise, was nowhere in sight. Even his dust had settled. The only thing I could do was keep going fast, realizing that our little group was now strung out over a dangerously long distance.

We had just about given up on seeing the grader again when we spotted it up ahead, stopped and off the road. The crew was standing next to a creek, pointing excitedly at something. We pulled along side as our third vehicle came to a screeching halt behind us. We all came together wondering what all the excitement was about and then we saw it. The largest snake I had ever seen, was sunning itself along side of the creek. We had to get closer. Our leader decided to see if the snake was alive. Without hesitation he pulled out his .45 caliber pistol and placed a shot in the mud beside its head. Not a move, not even a twitch. This snake is the soundest sleeper in the world, I thought, or it's dead. Guy-in-charge prods it with a stick. It was stiff, real stiff. We agreed to blow it away. I mean, after all, we can't have dead things cluttering up a war zone. So we ran back to the vehicles for our M-16 rifles, shotguns and anything else that went bang and plastered not only the snake but also the creek and the tree line next to it. We stopped only when we ran out of ammunition and were quite satisfied we had done our best to rid the area of a potentially dangerous health hazard. The ground was littered with empty cartridge cases and the terrain around us looked as though an armored division had passed by. It was a mess.

That evening, back at base camp, we were in the chow hall eating dinner with some buddies, recounting the snake story, when a couple of Army troopers stopped by and said they needed to talk with us. We moved aside to make room for them and they told us that just last night, they had been alerted that a group of several hundred North Vietnamese Army (NVA) regulars were believed to have been in the area. An aerial observer had seen evidence that a skirmish may have taken place about five miles down the road near a creek line. They asked if we knew anything about it. We shook our heads, no. Who did the shooting and what was the body count, was the big question on the Army's' mind. They warned us not to go down the road for the next several days until the situation settled down. After they left we just stared at each other, unable to believe how lucky we were not to have encountered the NVA, if in fact the intelligence about the enemy movement was correct. We all agreed never to mention the incident again while we were in Vietnam.

ABOUT THE AUTHOR: Dave Shill served with the Seabees in Chu Lai from April 1970 to April 1971. He holds the rank of Senior Chief Builder in the Naval Reserve and resides with his wife Lynne in Morristown, New Jersey.

THAT CERTAIN SMILE
By Joseph E. Gutierrez, M.D. F.A.C.S.

"Bac Si, Bac Si" - the voice was very soft, and the tug on my sleeve was so gentle that it seemed not to have happened. Then I heard the voice once more - "Bac Si" (doctor). I'd been standing on the crest of the hill above the Perfume River, just outside the gate of the provincial hospital in the old Imperial city of Hue. Across the river to the north was the old walled city, most of it now in ruins, after the Tet offensive of February 1968. I had stepped outside the hospital compound and gone across the street to view the river scene below me and the ramparts of the old Citadel across the river.

Turning around and looking at the source of the interruption of my reverie, I saw a tiny slip of a young girl; almost diminutive as the little baby she carried astride her left hip. The girl was probably ten or twelve, I surmised, and the infant she carried was probably a year and half or two. The pair of large dark eyes staring up at me were pleading, and the voice was plaintive. Again she spoke very softly and hesitantly, "Bac Si – please…" She then pointed to the baby's upper lip and the cleft lip was immediately obvious marring the innocence of that doll-like face.

It was late morning in early March of 1968. The day was beginning to warm up and I had been enjoying a brief respite from the morning's surgical schedule. There were no surgeons at the provincial hospital because they were all serving in the military. The thousand-bed hospital had over three thousand patients, many sharing the same bed. I had gathered a volunteer crew, and on 'off' days we would travel from Phy Bai to Hue in order to operate at the provincial hospital. And now here was this pre-adolescent girl, shyly mustering up the courage to beg a medical favor for her what… sister… cousin? I peered down at the children and the older girl could not seem to decide whether to stand her ground, or turn and flee. She tried to sense my moon… not easy, since I wore sunglasses and she could not expect what my reaction would be.

A candy bar always helps, and I slowly reached into my pocket, pulled out my 'emergency' candy bar, and slowly handed it to the young lady. Her eyes lit up (as did the baby's) but it took a bit of coaxing to convince her I really meant to give her the candy bar. That encounter over, I took her hand and led her across the street into the hospital compound where we sought out my interpreter.

The two girls were sisters, the interpreter explained, orphaned a few weeks previously during the battle for Hue. The sisters lived with their maternal aunt and various and sundry relatives in a makeshift house just on the outskirts of the city. It was the older sister's responsibility to watch over her baby sister, while older relatives tried to eke out what meager earnings they could in order to survive. The older girl was calm and cool, and we nicknamed her Jade. The baby had a couple of teeth showing through the cleft lip, and I called her Pearl. It was obvious that the baby did not have much of a future, given her deformity.

So Jade had decided to act on behalf of her sister. Having seen us drive into the hospital once or twice a week, she had finally mustered enough courage to ask for help. The interpreter thought she was being over-presumptuous; I thought we should proceed with the surgery.

We arranged to perform the surgery the following week. The Operating Room supervisor was to arrange the hospitalization, the surgery, and the instructions to the family. . Back at the lst Medical Battalion (lst Marine Division), my crew and I, and my best friend and fellow surgeon George, picked out appropriate instruments and fine suture material.

The surgery took place a week later, in less than ideal conditions, and in an operating room whose walls were pockmarked with bullet holes from the recent battle of Hue. But the outcome was successful and Pearl was sent home a few days after her surgery. As she got ready to leave, one of our corpsmen who had acted as our scrub nurse during surgery pulled out his Polaroid camera. He took a photograph of Jade and myself carrying Pearl, who had a lovely smile on her face and a nicely repaired lip. Jade clutched the photograph along with her baby sister, and then hugged me by the waist before they said good-bye. We never saw either child again.

A couple of months later, our unit was ordered back to Da Nang. I was part of the last group to leave Phy-Bai, and on our last day the 1st Med. hospital camp was almost totally deserted. Our interpreter came and sought me out and handed me a small brown bag, from Jade and Pearl she said. Inside the bag were a candy bar, to replace the one I had given, and a Polaroid picture of Jade and Pearl that they'd managed to get some Marine to take. The lip repair looked great, but the smile on both faces was the greatest reward. Jade and her family sent their thanks.

I asked the interpreter to take back a message: thanks for the candy bar... I'd keep it for 'emergencies'... but would they please keep the photograph... the image would stay with me forever.

ABOUT THE AUTHOR: Joseph (Joe) Gutierrez, was Chief of Surgery, 1st Medical Battalion, 1st Marine Division from November 1967 to November 1968. He currently resides in McLean, Virginia.

A GESTURE OF DEFIANCE
By Daniel C. Emke

In order for the true nature of this story be shared, it is necessary that one understand a major military axiom: Orders are to be followed under all circumstances. No questions asked. No 'ifs', 'ands' or 'buts'. When a superior gives you an order, you follow it. Not only is it to be followed precisely, if you are told to do it now, you do it now. No hesitation, just snap to and get it done. Months and months of basic training are spent molding "grunts" to instantly follow the orders of their superiors. The pretense of this training of course is to avoid any hesitation "under fire" which could prove costly in lives. I believe we all understand the basic premise, which is that if you're told to jump… you jump … without stopping to ask how high.

Corporal Dunbar was on his second tour of Vietnam. He was the leader of the 1st squad, 3rd platoon of "E" Company, 2nd Battalion, 5th Marines, and 1st Marine Division. Dunbar reminded me quite a lot of a famous soldier of another era, Sergeant Rock. He had the same square jaw and looked like he had a 5 o'clock shadow five minutes after he shaved. He was barrel-chested and had more chest hair than anyone I had ever seen, or since seen. He was an imposing figure. While he was probably no more than 22 years old, he looked as though he had been around, and in fact, he had.

It was March 1969. Our Platoon, the "third herd", was patrolling the lowland 20 miles southwest of Da Nang. Lieutenant Chipley, our platoon commander, rotated back to the States and we had welcomed our new Lieutenant the previous day. He was fresh from the States and this was to be his first patrol. It was obvious that contact was expected because the entire platoon was patrolling while the balance of the company maintained perimeter. Daytime patrols with a platoon usually meant trouble. It's not as if you could sneak-up on anybody moving through open terrain with thirty or so men. Then again, with daytime patrols of this size you weren't trying to sneak up on anybody, you were either out looking for something in particular or just trying to draw fire. A platoon stretched out and staggered made a mighty tempting target. You stretched the men out and staggered them to keep injuries to a minimum should one of the many hazards find some unlucky fellow. Communication passed along from man-to-man, mouth-to-mouth. It was a procedure that worked effectively. Usually.

It was about high-noon when we received rifle and automatic weapons fire from a village about 300 yards to our right. I'm not talking about an incoming shot or two from a sniper where you crouch down on one knee and look around for the little @#$##@$ so you can blow him away. I'm talking about bursts from automatic weapons that send you on your belly looking for cover and a sustained fire that gets you real familiar with the ground. Most of us found cover behind the paddy dikes but some of the men were behind mounds of dirt in the middle of the paddy wishing they could crawl over to the dikes. One of those men was Corporal Dunbar.

From experience I had learned that there were ways of handling the situation we were in. The most popular was to call in air support, let them rip the village to shreds, and then you assault, on-line, through the village killing what wasn't already killed by the air strikes. It usually took very little time to get support of some kind called in. You could do all this while you were laying down return fire. Or, if you wanted to get into it right away, you could start flanking maneuvers once your return fire squelched the enemy's initial advantage.

Well, we had a new Lieutenant on his first patrol, and under fire for the first time. The Platoon Sergeant who normally keeps close to the Lieutenant was stuck in a different paddy when the Lieutenant decided to take charge. Take charge fresh out of Officer Candidate School (OCS). I'm not saying anything derogatory about OCS training, but there are great differences between doing things under fire within the confines of a training exercise at, say, Camp Swampy USA, than in Vietnam. The enemy had real bullets.

The Lieutenant was lying on his belly behind a dike yelling for Corporal Dunbar. The mound of dirt that Dunbar managed to hide behind was directly between the Lieutenant and himself. He heard his name being called and stuck his hand up in the air and waved to show the Lieutenant where he was. He brought it back down quickly to avoid losing it to an enemy bullet. We could all see his hairy hand waving in the air. The Lieutenant had seen it too and yelled to Dunbar, "On my command, I want you to get your squad on their feet, get them on line and assault that village!" As I said earlier, experience had shown me various strategies for handling the situation we were in, and his orders weren't any of them. Remember, we were in the opening minute of a firefight, under sustained fire. We knew that the pressure would no doubt let up once we started to return fire, but this was the Lieutenants first firefight and he was anxious to prove himself.

Most eyes were now watching the mound in astonishment awaiting Corporal Dunbar's response. Immediately we saw the big hairy hand come up again. This time it was not waving. It was balled up into a fist with the middle finger fully extended. This universally accepted gesture of non-compliance is not your usual response to an order from an officer. However, Dunbar incorporated into one little gesture exactly what we were all thinking at the time. The Lieutenant had his better options explained to him later by the Platoon Sergeant, and I'm sure even he has a good laugh looking back through time at that hairy hand sticking up in response to his first combat order.

ABOUT THE AUTHOR: Daniel (DC) Emke was a squad leader in "E" Company, 2nd Battalion, 5th Marine Regiment, 1st Marine Division from January to May 1969. He resides in East Amherst, New York, with his wife Donna.

FIREBASE RIPCORD – A TRILOGY

By Major Charles F. Hawkins, U.S. ARMY Retired

Ripcord was the name given to a firebase set up by the 101st Airborne Division near the northeast rim of the Pi Shaw Valley in western Thua Thien Province. The base was a constant target of the north Vietnamese Army from latter 1969 well into 1970. It was as significant and costly an action as Hamburger Hill the year prior, but press coverage was tightly controlled.

In the end, Ripcord pitted four regiments of North Vietnamese regulars against the 2d Battalion, 101st Airborne Division, and parts of two other U.S. Battalions. The Americans fought a tough fight against long odds (one estimate was 10:1).

Still, the series of grim fire fights, vicious nighttime engagements, bloody patrol actions, and day-long battles around Ripcord were not enough to quench the human spirit. Despite 50 percent losses in the battalion, soldiers found time to joke, as well as cry. Years later, both humor and poignant memory remain equally clear.

RIGHT TWO FEET... DROP TWELVE FEET

Search and Destroy, East of Ripcord, July 14, 1970—During the period when Fire Support Base Ripcord was under siege by North Vietnamese forces (July 1-23, 1970), there was one particular artillery fire mission that stands out as remarkable.

The lesson the event teaches is that cooperation between different military services is limited only by the imagination, especially when fighting a determined enemy. I was there in the rugged reaches of jungle mountains in the northern I Corps Zone in Vietnam, and this is what happened.

Captain Dave Rich's artillery battery (Battery B, 2d Battalion, 319th Artillery, 101st Airborne Division) was the centerpiece of fire base defenses. Situated on the highest part of the 927-meter mountain, Rich's six 105mm howitzers and their crews had kept pace with the enemy's offensive. Fire missions were frequent, and occurred day and night. Anyone who had a target could request artillery fire and count on a quick response.

Rich's cannoneers were not only quick, but enjoyed a spooky reputation for accuracy. But with high-explosive projectiles that spewed lethal steel splinters over a 20- by 30-meter burst area, and could cause casualties as distant as 175 meters, accuracy was like horseshoes: the rounds only had to be close enough.

In most cases, artillery fire missions were called for by ground units in contact with the North Vietnamese, or by aerial observers in light helicopters. Control and use of artillery always remained within the Army hierarchy and artillery, infantry and helicopter units. Never was its use considered a joint operation where another service—the Air Force—might be involved.

But on July 14, all that changed. On that day, artillery fire support became a joint mission between Rich's troopers and Air Force Major Skip Little. The "redlegs" (artillerymen) on Ripcord faced a test of accuracy that was unheard of.

Little was a forward air controller, a FAC, who piloted the curious Cessna O-2A with its rear-mounted pusher and frontal puller propellers. The 0-2A was agile, and the rocket pods under its stubby wings held white phosphorous rockets for marking target locations for air strikes by F-4 Phantom jets.

In the clear sky over Ripcord, Little's observation craft wheeled and flew over an enemy bunker location that had just been struck by two Phantom jets. The jets had expended their ordnance on the target and broke station, returning to their base to rearm and refuel. Little was conducting a bomb damage assessment.

Suddenly, green tracer fire stabbed upward out of the dense forest, and fireballed past Little's Plexiglas canopy. With catlike reflexes, he hauled back on the stick and jerked his head around to see where the enemy fire had originated. The North Vietnamese machine gunner fired again, and .51-caliber tracers shot through the sky, dangerously close to the O-2A. This time, Little pinpointed the bad guy's location—a cave in the side of a rocky ridge facing the fire base about two kilometers away.

With no jets on station, and none due soon, Little radioed the tactical operations center (TOC) on Ripcord, and announced that he had a target; if the artillery would like to shoot at it, he would adjust fire.

Normal, high-angle artillery fire wouldn't do the job, Dave Rich realized he would have to employ a howitzer in direct fire in order to get rounds into the mouth of the cave. But from their firing positions on top of Ripcord, the tubes of the 105mm guns couldn't be depressed low enough to shoot the target. One of the howitzers would have to be moved to the edge of the hill, its tails propped up on ammo boxes and sand bags, to achieve the desired line of sight depression.

This was quickly accomplished, and Rich radioed his readiness to fire Little's mission.

In response, Little released one of his white phosphorous rockets to mark the target. It burst near the cave, which gave Rich a starting point. In a few seconds, two 40-pound projectiles went streaking downhill into the jungle toward the mouth of the cave. Little called back an adjustment, and Rich's men fired again. The high-explosive rounds struck closer this time, but the cave mouth represented a small target. Little radioed another adjustment; the rounds hit still closer, but no close enough.

"You almost got it," Little radioed. "Now, bring 'em right two feet and drop twelve feet."

Break. Adjustments to artillery fire are always given in meters, the smallest increment used is 25 meters, but usually a 50-meter adjustment will suffice. No one in the Army gives corrections in terms of "feet", but how could one expect an Air Force FAC to know this. Could the cannoneers possibly make such a small change to the leveling bubbles on the gun sight?

Rich and his redlegs "Rogered" Little's adjustment request without a second's hesitation, and two more rounds cannonballed toward the enemy machine gunner and his cave.

"That's a direct hit!" Little radioed with excitement. "Right into the mouth, both of 'em." The fire mission was over.

"Hot damn," I thought to myself at the time, "that is some kinda' good shooting.

Four months and some hard fighting later, and after Dave Rich had recuperated from wounds he received on Ripcord, I finally found the opportunity to remind him of the event and ask how he had managed to pull it off. Dave looked at me for a moment, his eyes twinkling as he recalled the event. "Simple," came his laconic reply, "just lean against the tube and spit down the bore."

A score-plus years later, I can't think of a more reasonable answer.

HO CHI MINH... THE DOG

Camp Evans Rear Base, December 1970—Wherever you find soldiers, sailors, airmen or marines, there, too, will be pets of various persuasions. Serving a variety of functions, from simple companionship to entertainment and even to aid in fighting a relentless foe, members of the animal kingdom—domesticated as well as wild, are as ubiquitous to warfare as guns and bullets.

A certain Colonel I recall had a duck at his brigade headquarters in Vietnam, which, it was mongered about, rated a salute from soldiers passing by.

The Vietnam War saw its share of pets more useful than ducks, and on both sides. The North Vietnamese were rumored to have elephants carrying supplies in our northern, mountainous area of operations. Although I never laid eyes on an enemy pachyderm, we were under orders to engage them with light anti-tank weapons, should the opportunity present itself.

Scout dogs bring back memories, and although they could sniff out the enemy at 800 meters or more, if the wind was right, they tired just like human soldiers after a hot, humid hump over jungled peaks and valleys. Dogs were also a common feature in rear areas.

Our infantry battalion had a mongrel mascot, affectionately named Ho Chi Minh and shortened to "Ho'Ch." He apparently understood his special status, because he regularly conducted inspections of subordinate mascot mutts at the different company orderly rooms.

Good old Ho'Ch had a Labrador retriever somewhere in his ancestry, and was larger than typical Vietnamese dogs. Black, with a white blaze running down his chest, he stood about knee-high, and had certain qualifications which endeared him to infantrymen and officers alike.

He could cook. Eggs, mostly, which he would carry tenderly in his mouth without breaking the shell until he found a flat rock, heated by the sun to near-frying temperature. Then, with the dignity and deliberateness of Julia Child, Ho'Ch would drop his raw egg on the rock—from just the right height to ensure it would break but not splatter—and wait for it to heat before dining. He seemed to prefer eggs "sunny-side up," but it was said he could use a spatula to cook them "over easy." Although I never saw this latter method.

He could tell time. After first call (Ho'Ch bunked with the warrant officer in charge of battalion maintenance), mornings were invariably spent in breakfast meetings along the company street. At 1200 hours sharp, he would appear at the officers' mess for the noon meal, and at 1400 he was always ready to accompany the battalion executive officer on his inspection of bunker line defenses.

Eventually, Ho'Ch's performance of duty earned him the rank of sergeant, E-5, but he never won the coveted Combat Infantryman's Badge. Afraid of the sound of guns firing, he always tucked his tail and skedaddled whenever shots were heard. Of course, that could have just been canine wisdom.

Most memorable was the time Ho'Ch faced down an abusive guest in the officers mess. There was always a place reserved for Ho'Ch at the dining table, and when he joined the officers at noon and jumped up on his chair, the mess steward promptly prepared and served him eggs and bacon. This particular day, Ho'Ch sat at the end of the table between me and a visiting helicopter pilot. The Army aviator, a junior warrant officer, offered what he probably meant to be a humorous observation about "dogs at the dining table." Ho'Ch, however, didn't find the remark funny. He stopped eating his eggs and bacon and fixed the aviator with an unblinking stare.

"Why's he starin' at me like that?" the warrant asked.

"You've insulted him," I said. "He'll keep it up until you apologize or move."

"You gotta' be kiddin'," came the airman's incredulous reply. "I'm not apologizin' to a dog. Are you guys serious?"

"Doesn't matter about us," I answered, "we like resupply helicopter pilots just fine. Ho'Ch is the one who's upset by your remark, and he's serious."

Now aware that an uncomfortable situation had developed at our end of the mess hall, fellow officers kept up a casual chatter, but everyone's third eye and ear were tuned to what might happen.

The warrant officer tried to shrug it off and shoved a bite of food into his mouth. Ho'Ch glowered at him, unmoved and unmoving, one paw beside his plate, the other on his chair. It was a hand-on-hip stance evocative of a schoolmarm confronting an errant child. No one came to the warrant officer's rescue; Ho'Ch, on the other hand, needed no help.

In a matter of seconds—long seconds they must have seemed to the uncomfortable aviator—it was over. He could stand Ho'Ch's scowl no longer, and with a grumble, got up and moved his plate and person to a place at the far end of the mess.

Satisfied, Ho'Ch immediately resumed his meal. But as he bent over to eat his eggs, he half-turned to me and winked: "Got him."

IN MEMORY OF TOM SHEPHERD, Oakton, Va., February 1992

Dear Mr. Shepherd,

Today I received word from John Mihalko of your son's death from cancer. I am so very deeply saddened; mere words simply can't say what my heart feels. I knew Tom Shepherd. I didn't just serve with him, I fought by his side over 21 years ago in Vietnam.

100

Tom was the medic for 2d Platoon, Charlie Company, 2d Battalion, 506th Airborne Infantry, 3rd Brigade 101st Airborne Infantry Division—the famous Screaming Eagles. I was assigned as platoon leader of that platoon in March 1970. Tom was part of my platoon command post (CP). He was part, an integral part, of a four-man team that ran the platoon day-to-day. Tom was with me-next to me—in my first firefight with the enemy; an experience seared into the memory of every combat veteran.

Take justifiable pride in your son's accomplishments, they were the stuff of legends. Tom was a true hero in every sense of the word. He was also a leader of men, and a champion of the less fortunate. He was reliable, steadfast and courageous. He was a man of valor, and while I have known many men of such quality, I have known none finer, or more brave.

Tom and I renewed our association in the fall of 1986 at a Ripcord Reunion in Whippany, New Jersey. For me, it was a happy surprise (and I think, also for him) for us to meet after all the intervening years.

I hope you will find the following personal recollections of Tom's service to his country of interest. They are supported by archival documents and from my letters home at the time.

I joined the 2d Platoon March 9, 1970. The platoon was participating in a series of operations to disrupt enemy infiltration into the populated coastal plain north of the old imperial Vietnamese city of Hue. The monsoon rains had begun to wane, and the partially clearing weather permitted us to move westward into the first line of rugged mountains that lie east of the A Shau Valley. Opposing us were members of the North Vietnamese 612th Sapper Battalion, and soldiers of the North Vietnamese 6th Independent Regiment. They were tough, seasoned veterans, and would give us a fight whenever they could.

Specialist Fourth Class Tom "Doc" Shepherd was one of the first men in the platoon that I met with and shook hands. The outgoing platoon leader was a West Point classmate of mine, Charlie "Tuna" Lieb, and he and 2d Platoon had established a reputation for toughness and courage under fire. As the new guy in charge, I knew that a lot would be expected of me, and that I would have to measure up. The other guys in the CP were Platoon Sergeant Queen (Queenie), the radio/telephone operator (RTO) SP/4 Rainwater, a southerner from Georgia.

The platoon was situated on a finger that came off a larger mountain ridge. Nearby was a small helicopter landing zone (LZ) where the platoon received a resupply of food, water and ammunition, and most importantly, mail from home. The LZ, and the comings and goings of the resupply helicopter, attracted the attention of some unwanted guests—North Vietnamese soldiers.

Early in the afternoon of March 11 (a Wednesday), the men in the platoon defensive perimeter were standing watch, cleaning weapons, and taking care of personal hygiene. Doc Shepherd had made his rounds a couple of time to ensure that everyone had taken the daily antimalaria pill, and to check on assorted nicks and cuts from jungle vines that we all suffered from time to time. Back at the CP in the center of the perimeter, Doc, Queenie, and I were playing a game of cutthroat pinochle.

It was a fun, relaxing way to relieve the combination of stress and boredom that every combat veteran knows. We were sitting on our upturned camouflaged steel helmets, and using an acetate-covered map as a playing surface. I had noticed that Doc didn't carry a weapon, but that he had three hand grenades inside his helmet; like a bird on a nest of eggs—some eggs.

I asked Doc why he didn't carry a weapon, but did carry hand grenades. He explained that he wasn't a conscientious objector, but that he considered himself a rather poor shot, and that during a firefight he was usually too busy worrying about wounded men to return fire anyway. The hand grenades, he stated, were easier for him to use if he got in a tough spot while tending a wounded buddy.

Sergeant Queen, perhaps sensing my concern that a man should have a rifle, nodded agreement with Doc: "He's right, Ell Tee (meaning LT for lieutenant). Doc's a tough one in a fight. Seen him go after more'n one down man with the bullets flying. He won't ever let you or the platoon down."

Queenie won the next hand, and as Doc was marking the scores, we heard the muffled "thonk, thonk, thonk" of enemy mortars firing about 100 meters away. All I could think was: My first firefight has just begun.

If you've ever been in a fire fight, you know that it's a crazy, chaotic thing; nothing ever seems to happen the way you think it should, or the way it's shown in movies. One minute we were sitting around doing the routine things soldiers do, the next minute all hell breaks loose, and fear and adrenaline levels go sky high. Enemy mortar shells began crashing and exploding everywhere, mostly around the LZ. Queenie jumped up and headed for the sector of the perimeter he thought was receiving fire. I was frozen, trying to remember what it was lieutenants were supposed to do when stuff like this happened.

Doc was quick on his feet, grabbing his aid bag and his helmet full of grenades. Quickly, realizing that he couldn't wear the helmet with the grenades in it, he scooped them out and handed them to me. "Here, sir," he said, "you'll need these more than me," and he ran toward the sound of guns firing.

In the days and weeks that followed there were other firefights, night ambushes, and helicopter combat assaults into new places deeper in the mountains. Sergeant Queen was reassigned out of the platoon and Sergeant Thompson Foret, one of the squad leaders, became the new platoon sergeant.

In the first 10 days of April, the company, along with the rest of our battalion, fought a series of bloody, grueling actions against a determined enemy for control of a 1,000-meter-high hill we would later make into a fire support base called Ripcord. On April 9, we were finally given the mission to conduct a ground attack to secure the hill the next day.

Before dawn on Friday, April 10, the company was up and moving to platoon and then squad release points halfway up the mountain. Concentrations of artillery preparatory fire thundered and boomed, and Cobra attack helicopters circled high overhead as we made the final assault over the crest of Ripcord. By 0730 hours we were in control, Ripcord belonged to us and the enemy faded into the jungle where he would regroup to fight another day. Doc Shepherd was with us every step of the way—aid bag, 90-pound rucksack, hand grenades, but no rifle.

On April 11, when we were concentrating on digging foxholes and bunkers, and stringing concertina wire around the hill, disaster struck. The 2d Platoon CP needed a bunker and fighting position dug. SP/4 Denny Heines had volunteered to help Sergeant Foret, Doc and Rainwater at the CP. (I had been temporarily given duties as the company commander and was at the company CP about 50 meters away.) The weather was hot, the sun bright in a near cloudless sky. Most guys were in tee shirts working doggedly on foxholes or keeping guard with machine guns.

Ripcord had been a fire support base the year before, and had been abandoned as the winter monsoons forced a reduction in combat operations. Some former occupant, too lazy or careless, had buried a half-dozen hand grenades in his foxhole before leaving the year prior. That old foxhole, now filled in, was the exact location where Denny Heines was helping to dig the 2d Platoon CP position.

Denny was up to his chest in the six foot by foot-and-a-half trench. Just a few more inches of dirt to scoop out and he could call it a foxhole. He shoved the tip of his D-handle shovel into the bottom of the hole and felt it strike a hard object. He placed his foot firmly on the shove, pushed hard, and felt the earth give way. Then, when he lifted the blade-load of dirt, there was a grenade; a live hand grenade that his shove tip had activated by slicing off the safety pin. Denny had the shove at chest level, ready to dump it on the side of the foxhole when the grenade exploded.

Everyone on the hill heard the explosion, but Doc Shepherd was the first man on the scene. I got there moments later along with Foret and Rainwater. Denny was a bloody mess of puncture wounds from grenade fragments, and burned, torn skin from the blast, but he was still alive and fighting for his life. Doc worked quickly and feverishly, shouting orders between life-giving breaths to Denny's bloody mouth. He needed plastic, a poncho to cover and seal Denny's sucking chest wounds. He was pumping Denny's chest with one hand to keep his heart going. Rainwater had called for an urgent helicopter med-evac; someone had come up with a litter.

The med-evac chopper arrived quickly, speeding from stand-by at our Camp Evans rear base, and hovered into Ripcord. In that time Doc had gotten Denny stabilized, but was still giving him mouth-to-mouth resuscitation. Denny would live as long as he kept receiving life-giving breath from his fellow soldier.

As Denny and the stretcher were lifted into the waiting helicopter, the critical transfer of life support between Doc and the medic on the chopper took place. Doc motioned to Denny's chest and made signs to continue giving mouth-to-mouth. He tried to no avail, to shout the instructions over the roar of the helicopter's turbine engine.

Maybe the chopper medic didn't understand, or was a new guy and didn't know. Maybe he was overcome by the sight of Denny's bloody torso and face, and of Doc, also covered with the blood of his patient. In any case, the chopper medic made no motion to continue the first aid.

Doc tried to climb aboard, but the chopper was on an urgent mission, and lifted away. It hovered above Ripcord for a second, and then spun toward our secure base camp in the lowlands, and the battalion aid station. Doc was screaming now, cursing at the departing chopper. Denny would die if the first aid he had started was not continued. Doc grabbed me: Do something, sir! They don't know what they're doing!"

I tried. Rainwater gave me the radio and I called the battalion operations center; I told them to call the chopper pilots and have their medic breathe for Denny, to push his chest to keep his heart going. It was too late. SP/4 Denny Heines was already dead—"died enroute," was the radio report we got back.

It was a bad day. A sad day. Doc had almost pulled off a miracle, but some greenhorn medic had blown it. He was inconsolable, his tears mingled with Denny's blood, and he looked like a wild man. We were all in a dour, sullen mood. There is no good thing to come of war, and Denny's death reminded all of us how human, and vulnerable, we really were.

I didn't work with 2d Platoon after we left Ripcord to the defense of others. I was promoted to captain in late May and took over command of Alpha Company—that is another story.

However, I did stay in touch. I had friends in Charlie Company, and when the battalion got to the secure base area in the rear, I would visit my old outfit to say hello. When we were on operations in the field around Ripcord, I would occasionally listen to radio messages from the men of Charlie Company as they talked to the battalion operations center, or to Lieutenant Colonel Andre Lucas, the battalion commander (who was killed by enemy mortars on July 23d).

On July 1, Fire Base Ripcord began taking enemy mortar and recoilless rifle fire. Resupply choppers were shot at and hit. The North Vietnamese had encircled Ripcord with an infantry division, but we didn't know at that time how strong the enemy force really was.

During the day on July 1, Charlie Company was directed to occupy defensive positions on top of Hill 902, two kilometers west of Ripcord. Two platoons, the 2d and the 1st did so, while the 3d Platoon was sent to Ripcord for a "day of rest." Some rest, in the midst of rocket and mortar attacks.

That night—after Doc Shepherd had tended to the medial needs of 2d Platoon and had bedded down on the jungle floor to sleep— an enemy sapper unit crept silently toward the Charlie Company perimeter. It is not possible to know how many enemy soldiers there were. Some reports indicate about 40, others say it was higher, as many as 100. The truth is probably somewhere in between: Thirty sappers to penetrate the G.I. defenses… Thirty riflemen to provide covering fire outside the American perimeter.

Early in the morning of July 2, I was awakened and called to the radio by my Alpha Company RTO. We were on Fire Base O'Reilly, nine kilometers north of Ripcord, and even farther from Hill 902. Still, we could hear the radio messages from Charlie Company quite clearly. They were in serious trouble.

The North Vietnamese had gained the element of surprise, and were among the defending Americans before many knew what was happening. Some G.I.s mistook the sound of exploding satchel charges for bursting mortar rounds. These men took cover in their foxholes, which sappers eliminated one-by-one. Other men, who realized what was happening, formed into teams of two and three men, and set about the deadly task of hunting down the enemy. Rifle fire from U.S. M-16s and enemy AK-47s chattered back and forth across Hill 902. Exploding grenades and satchel charges punctuated the night. Illumination rounds fired from mortars on Ripcord lit the night with a flickering, strobe-like light, giving the defenders an advantage in finding and killing their tormentors. I can attest to how grisly and eerie the battle must have been.

In the end, Charlie Company prevailed, but at a terrible price. Eight men, including the company commander, Captain Hewitt, lay dead, and about three times that number were wounded. The enemy had paid dearly as well, and their dead littered the slopes of Hill 902; numerous blood trails told of others being dragged off into the jungle.

It was probably this fire fight where Doc Shepherd was wounded, receiving multiple fragment wounds while going to the aid of his fallen comrades in Charlie Company.

After the Cambodian incursion by U.S. forces in April-May 1970 Ripcord, beginning on March 12, and lasting until July 23, was the next largest action of that year. In the final days, our battalion suffered over 60 dead and more than 340 wounded—roughly half our strength. The name "Ripcord," however, is graven in stone on the base of the 101st Airborne Division Monument at the entrance to Arlington National Cemetery, just south of the Potomac River from our nation's capital, Washington, D.C.

I hope this letter helps a bit, Mr. Shepherd. It helps me to write it, to let others know what it was like, to share what Tom and his fellow veterans went through. I'll miss Doc Shepherd, and I'll say a prayer for him, but he's in good company, really good company—the best a generation of America had to offer.

God Bless Chuck Hawkins

Post Script: There be of them that have left a name behind them. And some there be which have no memorial ... Their bodies are buried in peace; but their name liveth for evermore. -Ecclesiastics, XLIV, 8-14.

ABOUT THE AUTHOR: Charles (Chuck) Hawkins served in the 101st Airborne Division first as a platoon leader in "C" Company, 2nd Battalion, 506th Infantry Regiment, then as company commander of "A" Company. He resides in Oakton, Virginia with his wife Glenda and holds the rank of Major in the retired reserves.

DREAM ON
By Paul L. Bennett, U.S.N. Retired

I had been stationed on a remote island off the coast of Vietnam for about six months as the Senior Naval Advisor to the newly organized Vietnamese Junk Force when BMCM (Master Chief Boatswain's Mate) Buchiarelli reported for duty. The Advisor's job involved teaching the fledgling Vietnamese Junk Force's officers and enlisted crewmen how to prevent the Viet Cong from moving supplies and men up and down the coast. The Advisors accompanied the five man enlisted crews on patrols on 50-foot long boats called Jabutas. The boats were armed with fifty caliber machine guns and each crewman had a personal weapon. The routine consisted of stopping, boarding and inspecting the many fishing and merchant vessels traveling the coast of Vietnam. Our detachment was responsible for about 37 miles of coastline and for all of the rivers and tributaries within that area. The patrols were normally 48 to 72 hours in duration but seldom produced anything of great importance. The Advisors were not trained to speak Vietnamese in the early days of 1965 and neither did the Vietnamese speak English. Communication was accomplished by a mutual understanding of French, by drawing pictures or by body language and voice inflection.

The patrols were long, boring, frequently upsetting to the stomach and always lonely. BMCM Buchiarelli was relieving BMC Boyle who had finished his year in-country. It was good timing because Chief Boyle probably could not have lasted another week. His year had been spent in fear, and he had used alcohol, at lot of it, to somewhat dim his nightmares. Lately, everything was getting to him… the food, deprivation, heat, monsoons, Viet Cong, the lack of showers, electricity and even the lack of American conversation. Probably on the top of the list should be the snakes. Boyle cringed every time he even thought of snakes, and the Island was loaded with them. A Bamboo Viper had been killed inside the living quarters earlier in the week and a four-foot snake had shed its skin under Boyle's cot a month before. Boyle had remained drunk for most of the last month in anticipation of his return to the States and also because of his belief in the superstition about the enhanced likelihood of getting killed in the first or last month of the tour.

BMCM Buchiarelli settled into the daily routine cautiously as he spent the next few days listening to all the warnings issued by Chief Boyle and the tips about how to remain alive until the same time next year. Each morning the Advisors would be up at 0600 even though nothing might be scheduled for that day. An Advisor's role was whatever each made of it. Some had little to do with their counterparts except to report when they were not performing their jobs properly. As the only American Officer assigned, I tried to have a good working relationship with the Vietnamese and assist their Officers whenever and however I could.

Buchiarelli took the normal time that any Advisor took to begin his short timers calendar - one day! Everyone developed some kind of system to record the passage of time. Some had 52 malaria pills in a bottle and each week would make a ritual of popping the pill and chalking off another week from their tour. Most individuals used a real, calendar with their own special system of marking it. Special days, like the first and last hundred days, required some kind of celebration to mark the event. It took about a week for Buchiarelli to begin to question why we were pulling a 0600 reveille when nothing happened until 0800. It was apparent from the beginning that the Master Chief was a wheeler dealer who felt that rules were made to be broken. He approached me one night, after we had finished supper with the Vietnamese Officers, and began by posing a series of simple questions.

"Sir, how long is the tour in Vietnam?"

Answer: "One year."

"Can it be shortened?"

Answer: "Yes, get killed or lose a limb."

"Is there any other way? What if I get wounded or get sick?"

Answer: "All taken care of in-country.

"How about if I get malaria, yellow fever, dysentery or the clap or VD?"

Answer: "No way, Master Chief, they're all handled in-country. There is no way to get out of the country unless you're carried out. The sick and wounded get treated here, in-country. You spend the whole 365 days here or go out in a body bag, so stop screwing around. You might have beat every other system but you are not going to beat this one!" I said, getting a little annoyed.

The Master Chief went off to the Village to drink some warm Ba Mui Ba beer and contemplate his next strategy.

Several days later, shortly after 0600, while I was washing up out of the 55-gallon drum that we had for that purpose, Buchiarelli screamed, "I got it! I got it! This is beautiful, just .beeoootiful! Lieutenant, wait till you hear it!" The Master Chief ran into the wash area knocking over the beer cans which had been strung on cat gut to warn of Viet Cong. The quarters that the Advisors shared didn't have modern conveniences like door or windows so they were constantly devising rudimentary warning devices. "Lieutenant, I got it. I can get out of this dump in eleven months, maybe even ten! It's so simple I can't believe it."

"Master Chief, get off my ass. You're still drunk from last night."

"No shit, Sir. No shit! Listen, just listen! Lieutenant, can we sleep in until eight? There's not a thing going on anyway. We're the only ones awake at six. What the hell for?"

"Because six is reveille all over the Navy, and it's routine. It's one of the few things in my life that hasn't changed and it helps me hang on to my sanity. It's regulation and it makes sense in a senseless job. That's what the hell for, Master Chief."

"But, Sir. If you'll excuse me, Sir, that's bullshit. There's no one anywhere near here except the Slopes, and they sleep in 'til at least seven and then they take a friggin' three hour 'nooner' that we never take. Even on patrol there's three asleep in the deckhouse and two sleeping on the goddamn tiller. Those guys are always asleep and it's their war! "

"Master Chief, what is the big deal? You hit the rack every night by ten or eleven. We've got no T.V., no entertainment - all we can do is read by lantern and you haven't even read a funny book yet. How much goddamn sleep do you need?"

"It ain't the sleep, Sir. It's the friggin' tour! If I get to sleep 'til eight I can knock a month off the hitch."

"Now how in the hell do you do that? You're as bad off as Boyle and you've got less than a month in-country. You've never even been shot at and you're already losing it. What the hell are you talking about?"

"Sir, listen, just listen. How much is two hours times 365 days? It's seven hundred and thirty hours, Sir. Seven hundred and thirty divided by twenty-four is over thirty days and thirty days from three hundred sixty-five days is three hundred thirty-five days. Now doesn't that make sense, Sir?"

"Buchiarelli," I shouted, "You get one more chance. What the hell are you mumbling about?"

"The tour, Sir! The friggin' tour! If I can sleep in till 0800, I only do eleven months instead of twelve!"

"How in the name of Christ did you ever make E-9, Buchiarelli? You're still here for twelve months - it doesn't make a bit of difference how much you sleep!"

"No, Sir. Can't you see? When I'm asleep, I'm not here. I'm a great dreamer, Sir. I'm back in the North End of Boston, going to the Red Sox, seeing the Bruins. I'm never, ever here when I'm asleep, Sir."

"Buchiarelli, get the hell out of here. Go take a walk, go for a swim. Do anything! But get out of here!"

"You just think on it for awhile, Sir. You'll be able to figure it out," Buchiarelli said. He mumbled to himself as he walked away, "How did they ever make that dumb shit an Officer?"

ABOUT THE AUTHOR: See "The Cave".

SHORT TIMER - COMBAT PUPPY
By Alan L. Fuchs

I met Short Timer for the first time on Hill 54 in South Vietnam in late 1967. It was an odd meeting in a hard rain during the monsoon season. A group of us stood on a small hill, discussing gun emplacements for our 105mm Howitzers. Suddenly, something on the ground between my legs caught my eye. A little flack nose and two warm brown eyes looked up at me from under my gear. Something had sought refuge under me from the rain. Jumping back, I saw a golden brown puppy wet to the bone standing in the mud. All the guys laughed about how I jumped away from the little creature. "What's his name, Al?" they asked.

I thought for a minute. "Short Timer."

I picked him up, put him back under my rain gear, and took him to my wet bunker. Everything was soaked, but I found a dry spot up high on the sandbags. I dried him off as best I could, cleaning and checking him out in the process. His eyes were clear, but he still shivered. Taking off my rain gear, I stuffed the little guy into my jungle fatigue jacket next to my body. I was shivering too, but at least we could shiver together. As I leaned back,. he laid across my stomach… seemingly content. We just stayed that way for a while, both of us just looking at each other. What was he doing there in the middle of a war zone? Could he even understand my English? I opened a can of C-rations and offered him some, but he turned his nose up. "Smart dog," I thought. "Nobody else likes the ham & eggs either." However, I had a can of Spam from my folks back home which he ate without hesitation.

"Listen," I said to Short Timer, "We are in a war zone, understand? You're going to have to go back where you came from, you hear? On a United States Military Fire Support Base you are definitely against regulations." I looked outside. It was still cloudy and overcast, but the rain had stopped. I picked him up, took him over to the perimeter barbed wire and put him on the ground. "Go home!" I said with a stern voice pointing beyond the barbed wire. He just sat there looking at me. It's dangerous here. People die here. What if... and besides, who is going to take care of you anyway? You're going to have to find your own way. You live here! Someday, if I'm lucky, I'll go home too. Then what'll happen to you?"

I turned away from him and walked toward the gun pit. At the sandbag wall, I looked back and he wasn't there. I didn't see him until I looked down at my right side. Short Timer was sitting there looking up at me. "OK," I said, giving in to his gaze, "but you'll have to listen-up when I talk."

As the days passed he followed me everywhere. Strangely, though, he never played or showed any emotion, which is kind of unnerving from a dog. At night I would pull phone watch, in case the infantry out in the "bush" needed artillery support. Short Timer would sit next to me and look out into the darkness, for the enemy I guess. We both knew the North Vietnamese Army was out there somewhere. Some nights we would hear gunfire in the distance. On other nights the ground under us would tremble, and we'd hear the deep rumbling sound of a B-52 bomb run. Towards the end of the monsoons, we got some clear nights. I would look up at the stars while his ears continually panned back and forth, nose sniffing the air. It was quiet and peaceful. Since most of the infantry was out on patrol at night, we had to pull guard duty ourselves. I'd pick up the M-60 machine gun and the M-79 grenade launcher, my M16 rifle, a 38 caliber S&W pistol in my shoulder holster, a large hunting knife on my belt, with bandanna's of ammunition slung across over my shoulders, dressed in jungle fatigues, combat boots, a flack jacket, and helmet, looking like I'm going to end the war in Vietnam. And there, by my side, was a puppy dog. We were two mean dudes.

At the guard bunker I'd do a communications check on the phone to let the men know I was in position. I rearranged the sandbags so Short Timer had a hole to look through. If he sat on top where we looked out, the local sniper could pick him off. Short Timer never made a sound and we would read each other's body language, communicating with our eyes. Sometimes during the night, especially on the dark nights, he would move close to me and lick me.

One night during phone watch on the gun, a big rat came into the gun pit, as big as an alley cat. I was leaning back, resting my head against the sandbags and didn't see it. Suddenly, the rat jumped on my face and Short Timer went after it. It was twice the size of Short Timer, but they scuffled in the dirt with Short Timer growling and biting the rat. He got bitten a few times himself, but the rat decided it was too much for him and scurried away. I got on the phone and called the Sergeant to get Doc up to my gun right away. The medic came running with his bag. The other guys on the guns saw Doc running and came over too. Short Timer was bit pretty bad, so Dock took care of his wounds while a little crowd gathered around Gun 2. Then the Top Sergeant (who was also known as the Chief of Smoke) came up. "That's a pretty mean dog you got there," he said holding up a dead rat that was all of two feet long! He had found it on the way up to my gun. Short Timer was only a puppy, I told him. "Well, it must have been him that killed it," the Top Sergeant continued, "There's a blood trail from where I found it all the way up to his gun pit."

The medic bandaged Short Timer's wounds. For the rest of the night, he lay in my lap. I looked at him and said, "Rest easy my friend."

On another night in January 1968, the silence was broken by the beginning of the Tet Offensive. Our gun emplacement was taking a heavy barrage from a North Vietnamese Rocket battalion. At the onset of the first explosion, I took off my helmet and put it over Short Timer. No time to get him to a bunker. I went to my job on the Howitzer as number 1 man (loader). Locked into an artillery duel that lasted for 11 hours, I continued to load as we fired away. It wasn't until well into the next day when the guns went silent. We had taken heavy casualties. My gun had broken down due to the amount of firing, and I sat on the ground with my back up against a sandbag wall feeling strangely different, like when you wake up from a bad dream. I looked over and saw my helmet on the ground. Then I thought of Short Timer. My helmet was dented by the shrapnel and even had a bullet hole in it.

"You should have listened to me," I shouted at the helmet. "I told you to go home. But no, you wouldn't listen. You just wouldn't listen." Then the helmet moved. It moved again. I turned it over slowly and Short Timer was looking up at me. He was ALIVE! I picked him up and held him high in the air. "Welcome to the big leagues. You're a combat puppy now."

In the months to follow, I noticed how my battle weathered dog was teaching me how to use my senses. When we were airlifted to a new position, he rode the choppers with me. When we pulled guard duty, I would observe him, watching his body movements. He would look at me, keenly aware of his surroundings. I would gesture back with my eyes as he continued to scan.

One day, we were under heavy attack and were taking intense incoming mortar and automatic weapons fire. One of the men on my gun was badly wounded. The Med Evac helicopters were forced away by enemy fire, so we put the injured man in a makeshift bunker. Doc did what he could. Short Timer crawled on top of him and lay on his chest. That seemed to comfort the man. "Short will keep you company till the choppers come," I said. He smiled.

For what seemed like days, we waited. It was very early in the morning, still dark. The only light came from explosions outside the bunker. Suddenly, Short looked up with a quick movement. His hair stood on end. He rose, and backed off the man's chest. It was if he was watching something come through the bunker door. I looked, but nothing was there. Then, Short let out an unforgettable howl. "What the heck was that for," I said to Short.

"Angels, man, he saw the Angels," Doc said. Doc shut the man's eyelids that were open. He covered the man over with a blanket. Short Timer started to whimper and moved close to me. I put my arm around Short, and held him close. I said, "It's all right, Short, you did what you could, he's with the Angels now. We'll never forget him."

When the dry season came, keeping cool was paramount in everyone's mind, including Short Timer. His way was to dig a hole.

So that's where the idea came from to dig a fox hole. We were taking 10 salt pills a day. Short Timer got his salt by licking me. I was beginning to feel like a lollipop. When we were at Base Camp, some of the guys would take a truck and drive down Highway 1 to the base at Chi Al. The Seabee's had a large freezer. In that large freezer was ICE! That was more precious than gold. The guys would trade a few brass artillery shell casings for a 150 lb. block of ice then do the land speed record for a five ton truck back to the base camp before it melted. Now that was a trick. The temperature hovered around 120 degrees, and that was along the coast.

Well, Short and I would get a piece of ice, go on up to the communication bunker and listen to some good Motown sound that Chris Noel played on the Armed Forces radio station. We'd get real cool and relax, listening to Marvin Gay's "I Heard it Through the Grape Vine." Me and my iced Kool-Aid and Short with his iced water. Short would take a few licks, look up with a grin on his face. Gosh, he was one of the guys. I'd reach down and tickle his ears and say, "Just us men, right, Short?" He'd give me a look.

It was also during that time when we would tolerate each other's idiosyncrasies. After all, living together does sometimes create problems. We really didn't sleep deeply. We sort of cat napped, or should I say puppy napped? I got used to him walking around in the middle of the night. He also had the habit of snoring a little bit. He could often be seen lifting his leg on some guy's combat boots, which got him in a little trouble. "Maybe he likes you or something," I'd tell the unsuspecting soldier. Since Short Timer never complained anyway, I guess it's safe to say that I never got on his nerves. At least that's the way I'd like to think of it.

We served many missions together. We shared a lot. The last day I saw Short Timer was sometime in September 1968, when I became the short timer. I was out in the field when my orders to go home came. I wanted to bring Short Timer home with me. I went to the Chief of Smoke and asked him for papers to bring Short Timer home with me. "There are no papers for dogs. The military dogs don't even get to go home, never mind a mutt…" came the reply.

"Sarge, you don't understand!" I protested.

"Yeah, I do. If you're not on that chopper when it leaves, you might as well call this place your home, 'cause you ain't never getting out of here otherwise."

I decided to find Short Timer and take him home anyway. Even if the military wouldn't let me, I'd find a way. I searched frantically, but couldn't find him. I called and called. Then I realized Short Timer must be deaf from the artillery noise. I just couldn't leave my combat puppy there. I went from gun pit to gun pit, but nobody had seen him. I was down-hearted. As my chopper came into the loading zone, I wanted to keep looking but I had to go. I climbed aboard.

"Hey, dude, you're going home. This is your freedom bird. Why so sad? You're going home to your girl," the door gunner on the chopper said. I told him that my dog was out there somewhere. The chopper nosed down as we lifted off the pad, and rose slowly into the air. I was sitting with my legs hanging over the side of the helicopter, one hand holding on, the other hand gripping my M16 rifle. The chopper leaned to the left as we made one final sweep around Hill 54. The men on the ground waving goodbye and giving me thumbs up and the peace sign as we passed over the fire base for one last time. The door gunner yelled something I couldn't hear. The pilot swung to the right and over the adjoining hill. There on top of the hill was a dog.

"It's Short Timer!" I yelled. There he was standing on the top of a small knoll looking up. He was wagging his tail. With tears in my eyes I said "Goodbye my friend, be safe." The chopper flew off into the setting sun. I watched until I couldn't see him anymore.

Short Timer earned a place in my heart. He was my buddy. His love and devotion to man stands paramount in my mind. We shared something in a world where no one belongs. Me and one of God's creatures.

I have over the years wondered about Short Timer. Maybe he went up into the Central Highlands of the Annimite mountains and found a loving Meo or Taoih Montagnard family to live with. Maybe he even had a family of his own. Oh, I guess he's old or maybe dead. I'll never know, but in my mind he's still a puppy.

In that tour of duty, a puppy became a dog while a boy became a man. Short Timer taught me a lot. I'll miss him. He was the epitome of man's best friend. After all it was HE that taught ME how to become a Short Timer in Vietnam.

ABOUT THE AUTHOR: Alan (Big Al) Fuchs served in Vietnam in 1967-1968 with the 1st Battalion, 14th Artillery, Americal Division. He co-authored the book "Vietnam Our Story, One On One". He lives in Atlanta, Georgia, with his wife Lucille and Beagle "Ollie".

THE PURPLE HEART

By Lieutenant Colonel Robert W. Michel, U.S. Army Retired

There were roughly 220,000 Purple Hearts awarded during the Vietnam War for wounds suffered in combat. Each, undoubtedly, has a story attached to it. This is one of them.

Prior to mid 1967, before the introduction of the "Cobra" attack helicopter, aerial gunship support to the ground troops in Nam was provided by the "C" model U1T-1 (Huey) helicopter. On board weaponry was installed in a variety of configurations. At the risk of boring you with technical details, some specifics about armament are necessary to help you understand exactly what happened on this eventful occasion.

The most common weapon configuration on the "C" model Huey was a combination of M-60 machine guns and eight round 2.75inch rocket pods attached to pylons on each side of the aircraft. A make shift arrangement at best but better than nothing. Another version consisted of two, twenty-four round rocket pods, one on each side, and like many things military, it had a nickname. 'The Hog' delivered an impressive volume of firepower but had one big disadvantage. The location of the rocket pods on the airframe prevented the installation of pintle mounts for the two M-60 door guns, and that limited the traverse and up and down motion of the guns, an important safety feature. Instead the machine guns were secured from the ceiling of the helicopter by a long bungee cord, which let a door gunner cradle the M-60 on his knees and even swing it inside the helicopter if he chose to. You might say, "So what, no one is careless enough to do that". Oh no? Guess again. It happened all too *often,* almost killing the pilot and co-pilot on some occasions. "But how could someone consciously do that?" you ask. "Easy," is the answer. It was not uncommon for a door gunner to get, what is known in aviation circles as, 'target fixation.' The eyeballs lock onto a target, oblivious to the motion or attitude of the aircraft. In a steep turn, for example, it was easy for a door gunner to inadvertently traverse the machine-gun inside the aircraft while focusing on a target. An errant door gunner shot off the exterior door handle on my helicopter, three inches from my elbow, during just such a maneuver. I hated the arrangement but had to live with it.

On this particular day, I was lead "Hog" in a flight of four gun ships returning from a routine and rather lackluster mission along the Cambodian border. Our flight route happened to take us over the infamous Michelin Rubber Plantation notorious for being a Viet Cong stronghold. From one thousand feet above the terrain the plantation appeared quiet. No movement among the trees was visible. Via the intercom I casually announced to the crew, whose names, unfortunately, I can't recall, that we were about to cross over the plantation and to keep an eye open for anything that appeared hostile. A few minutes passed when the door gunner on the port side of the aircraft excitedly yelled over intercom,

"We're taking fire!"

I looked down and saw nothing. "From where?" I answered. "From the trees?"

I scoured the landscape and again, nothing. "Are any of you guys taking fire?" I radioed to the other three gun ships. "Negative!" they replied. I looked over my shoulder at the door gunner and keyed the intercom button, "OK... return fire if you've got a target" I wasn't convinced we were under fire, but what the hell, let the guy vent some pent up hostility. The machine gun clattered away.

Moments later the door gunner on the starboard side of the aircraft shouted, "He's been hit". I twisted in my seat and saw the other door gunner, who had been doing the firing, lying on the floor of the chopper withering in pain.

"Where, has he been hit?" I asked.

"In the foot!" he called back.

"OK, Get his boot off, wrap his foot in a bandage from the medical kit on the wall, and put a tourniquet around his leg." Looking back to the rear of the chopper I saw that he had already applied a tourniquet and was in the process of removing his boot. Deciding it was best to fly him to the hospital in Saigon, I radioed ahead for an ambulance to be waiting at the heliport and told the other gun ships to return to base.

When we landed, I shut the aircraft down and jumped out to help the ambulance crew lift the door gunner to the ground where a stretcher waited. As they put him on it, he looked up at me grimacing in pain and said, "Sorry for the inconvenience, Sir. As soon as I get this fixed, I'll be back."

"That's fine with me," I said to him admiring his spunk. For that matter, the vast majority of soldiers we had in Vietnam in the mid 60's were dedicated, tough and full of piss and vinegar. It was later in the war that attitudes changed, soured by growing dissatisfaction at home with the way the war was being handled. I was certain, however, that I had seen the last of my door gunner. He had, what in World War II parlance was called "the million dollar wound." A guaranteed one way ticket home.

I walked back to the helicopter to inspect it for bullet damage. It was clean except for some pools of blood on the floor of the cabin where the door gunner had been sitting. Out of curiosity, I picked up his boot from where it lay discarded and looked at it. Sure enough, there were the entrance and exit holes unmistakable in their appearance, except that the entrance hole was in the top of the boot and the exit hole was in the bottom. It was clear that he had unintentionally shot himself in the foot. We hadn't been taking fire from the rubber plantation after all. The wound was self-inflicted. It was that damned "Rube Goldberg" bungee cord arrangement that allowed it to happen. I said nothing to the other crewmembers and threw the boot in a trashcan near the helipad.

A month or so later, with the incident long since forgotten, I walked into company headquarters one morning to hear the company clerk say. "Remember so-and-so? The door gunner who got shot in the foot over the Michelin Plantation? He came back to duty last night."

"I'll be damned," was all I could say.

Ever few months it was customary in our unit to hold a formation on the airstrip to pass out medals to those who had earned them.

On this particular occasion the Brigade Commander himself came down to give our helicopter company a Valorous Unit Citation and individual awards to a select few. My door gunner stood proudly among others who were receiving awards and grinned with a sense of accomplishment as the Brigade Commander pinned the Purple Heart Medal on his fatigues.

I can picture him today sitting around the fire with his wide-eyed grandchildren reminiscing about his exploits in the Vietnam War. "There we were over the dreaded Michelin Rubber Plantation, receiving heavy fire from the ground. I had just nailed a few VC with my machine gun, when all of a sudden… etc… etc… etc…"

ABOUT THE AUTHOR: See "Rainbow Charlie".

WHY?

By Michael Young

There they were again, those two little girls. The tiny, round oriental faces, sprinkled ever so lightly with freckles, glowed with warmth when they saw me. Mischief illuminated their soft brown eyes, a clear reflection of the mirth within. We called them Titi and Beaucoup Mahp, "Little and Big Fat." The nicknames fit because they were pudgy little girls, unusual when you consider they were living in a time and place of war. But Vietnam was like that. There were those who were hungry, and those who were not.

Somehow, perhaps by jungle telegraph, they always knew when I was about to arrive in their little village of Tinh Binh, a tumble-down collection of shacks located some kilometers distant from the province capital, the City of Chau Doc. Tinh Binh is on the Vinh Te Canal, not far to the west of an abandoned set of locks we always negotiated with apprehension. We felt especially vulnerable to ambush as our U.S. Navy PBR's, thirty-one foot fiberglass patrol boats with little armor and not a whole lot of armament, passed through those narrow, earthen confines.

Sisters, Titi was four and Beaucoup was six. Less than three feet tall and a bit rotund, they brought to mind the classic image of ragged street urchins so often seen in old black and white movies. Since one was rarely ever seen without the other, it was often said they could easily have passed for twins if not for a six-inch difference in height. Although many felt they most closely resembled little gnomes, I thought other more unique qualities made them stand out from the ever-present crowd of kids who jammed the canal bank. They exuded a subtle but unwavering strength of character, and had a certain twinkle in the eye that hinted of wisdom beyond their years.

I didn't know the whereabouts of their parents, nor did I know if they were even alive. The two girls said very little about family, so I was left wondering if the parents might have been working for the enemy, the Viet Cong. There was a grandfather, a bit the village character, who wandered around most of the time stoned on something or other, usually extremely good pot. I was sure the old man was an embarrassment to his granddaughters because they carefully avoided talking about him.

The three lived in mild squalor with the girls' aunt, "Mamasan", in a humble hooch behind the small bar and refreshment stand she operated. Although I was unsure how they felt about Mamasan, I had no doubt how they felt about their grandfather. On those occasions when the old man would stumble past, the sisters would immediately fall in behind. I'd laugh, because the threesome always painted an unforgettable picture that of a long past-his-prime old rooster trailed closely by two chicks. The girls would stick close, until satisfied he was okay, and then quickly return to whatever they'd been doing.

I'd been trained to be fluent in Vietnamese, so I was able to communicate freely with the two sisters and had worked hard on developing a unique connection with them. Certain details of the relationship had to be kept secret, however, for I couldn't let anyone know they were the most select and best-informed intelligence sources I had cultivated in that area. Yes, I'd placed them at considerable risk. But they were brave. They recognized and accepted the danger, mostly, I think, because of a peculiar and deep loyalty to me. They had come to trust me without question, as I did them. We were friends.

That day, our boats had been assigned to patrol a specific section of the Vinh Te with orders to remain overnight in Tinh Binh. No night patrol had been designated, thank God, because those patrols could be the pits. Since the area along the Vinh-Te was semi-pacified, at least some of the time, patrols on that canal were often considered routine. Then would come the unexpected, and someone would die. When we'd completed the day's patrol, we returned to Tinh Binh and nosed the PBR's to the edge of the canal. The bank was steep there because it was deep into dry season and the water level was very low.

A horde of kids slid down the bank and rushed toward our boats. The two tiny gnomes were quite prominent among the crowd. Since those countless little mouths were always insatiably hungry, we drew on our supply of C-rations in an attempt to satisfy them. Most were remarkably greedy, but the two sisters politely waited until we got around to them. They never took much and always expressed their gratitude with a chorus of "thank yous" that still echo in memory. I split an extra packet of goodies between them, and then leaned over the side of the boat to give C-rations to a couple of others.

Suddenly, my favorite Zippo lighter fell from the upper pocket of my fatigues and dropped into the shallows at the canal's edge. Well aware of the Vietnamese' affection for money, I offered a few piasters (Vietnamese currency) to the kid who could find my lighter. With a remarkable burst of energy, all but the two sisters pretended an enthusiastic search. They just watched the activity, and especially my reaction, with undisguised amusement. It was evident they knew something I didn't and were taking considerable pleasure in keeping it to themselves.

After several minutes the search was abandoned, with no Zippo. I was at a loss to explain why nothing was found, for those kids could locate absolutely anything, anywhere, when money was the motivator. They also had an extraordinary ability to pick pockets without causing a ripple of suspicion, as I'd discovered on previous occasions. They were damn good.

Beaucoup Mahp caught my eye, and with the wiggle of a tiny finger invited me to come close. As I approached, the two little girls looked at each other and giggled. I knelt on one knee, but even then was looking just over their heads. I leaned closer. Beaucoup Mahp spoke softly into my ear. "Lieutenant, boy find your lighter and take to Black Market. There now… gone now."

Allowing for the delay with which comprehension dawned on Americans, she patiently explained the Zippo would bring a whole lot more than my offered reward when sold on the Black Market. She told me in her always-straightforward manner, and without trying to offend, that my offer simply wasn't sufficient, especially for the kid who'd found it. She wouldn't reveal his name.

So I went to Mamasan's bar for consolation. A fly-infested place, it was just some dusty spot along a narrow earthen lane that followed the canal bank, and was little more than about a hundred yards from our boats.

Mamasan was a woman in her thirties, hardly five feet tall, with broad and flat oriental features. She knew all the gossip in town, and a lot about enemy activity as well. She made me very uncomfortable, mostly because I sensed a genuine hatred of Americans behind her overly friendly facade.

The sisters refused to confirm or deny my suspicions and I never pressed the point. I respect loyalty, and over time I came to realize their loyalty to family was equal to their loyalty to me. So I'd hang around Mamasan's while the girls played at my feet and waited for an opportune moment to discreetly pass along their information. Since they never said anything about me to anyone, including Mamasan, I knew my secrets were safe with them.

I sipped my bug-infested beer and watched the Tinh Binh natives go through the motions of daily wartime life. I was amazed at the number of insects that could be sealed into a single bottle of beer, not to mention the awesome number that would fall or crawl into it.

I never wanted anything to eat, for a strong stench of decaying garbage always permeated the air. Flies buzzed incessantly and filth was everywhere. I detected a subtle undercurrent of fear in the place, as if no one dared speak freely or knew whom to trust.

I was on my second beer when I noticed the evening shadows were fast growing larger. Soon, the glow of candles and lanterns burning here and there in the village became the only evidence of life after sunset. The two sisters wished me goodnight and disappeared. I went down to the boats to get a little sleep, which I knew was going to be difficult, for the night was very hot.

An aurora of artillery fire was visible on the horizon, and once in a while the sound of exploding shells, highly muffled by distance, could be faintly heard. The remote low frequency booms recalled the rumble of distant summer storms so often heard in the muggy night air of my mid-western childhood home. I still remember how, in Vietnam, the least significant things would so often trigger the strongest memories.

Another officer and I decided to place a couple of cots on the canal bank because it was cooler there. We set them up close to the string of heavily barbed concertina wire that separated the dusty lane from the canal bank and our boats below. The night seemed quiet, so we bedded down.

About 3:30 in the morning I awoke with a start, for I'd felt the unmistakable tug of someone's hand. In the dim light I could see only that it was tiny, and connected to a short, pudgy arm which I followed directly to a trembling Beaucoup Mahp, her shadowy form nearly invisible in the darkness. Before she vanished into the murk, she whispered, "Get away Lieutenant. Now!" I woke the other officer and we both fled to the protection of our boats. I knew little Mahp so well I hadn't for a moment questioned the legitimacy of her warning.

Within no more than a minute a tremendous explosion split the night air and illuminated the narrow lane with a brilliant orange, and white flash that seemed to freeze all motion. Pieces of cot rained down, scattered across the decks of both boats and splashed into the canal around us. Since the explosion had occurred at the very spot where I'd been sleeping, I assumed we'd become a target. So we got underway at once, determined to avoid further attack. We figured we'd be less vulnerable if moving.

At first light we returned to Tinh Binh where Beaucoup Mahp stood waiting on the dock. The closer we came the more it was clear she'd been injured, so I jumped the few remaining feet between the bow of the boat and the bank, and ran to her. I drew her close and was appalled by what I saw. Her little shirt was bloodstained and one arm bore a deep laceration. Her face was scratched, and covered with small, black specks, so tiny they were impossible to distinguish from her freckles. Her clothes bore the heavy, acrid smell of cordite. I held her as we gently applied field dressings. She was cold and shivering, even on that warm morning. Her voice nearly a stutter, she attempted to tell her story. When she spoke, her swollen lips trembled uncontrollably.

It seemed two Viet Cong in the village had observed our placement of the cots. Suspicious they were plotting something little

Mahp had kept a careful eye on them. She had warned me as soon as she heard I was the target on my cot, then she withdrew undetected but stayed close by as the two VC lobbed a hand grenade directly at our cots only moments after we'd slipped away. She had continued to keep watch even though she'd been hit by several tiny pieces of shrapnel from the explosion itself. The razor-sharp concertina wire had cut her arm when she reached through to tug at me. I looked into those sweet brown eyes and felt, if only for a moment, the presence of someone or something very old, even ancient.

The little girl to whom I owed my life snuggled against me. I wrapped my arms more tightly about her in a feeble attempt to shield her from the suffocating sense of evil that seemed so close around us. Suddenly, I hated that place and everything in it. Then, as I felt warmth from the small form cradled in my arms; I realized how much I didn't want to hate at all. I heard Mahp's small, plaintive voice. It seemed to be coming from a terribly lonesome place and it bore a single word, awesome in its simplicity, yet one whose memory has never, ever gone away. You see, a courageous little girl had just asked me, "Why?"

ABOUT THE AUTHOR: See "Survivors".

A SKYHOOK FOR DANIEL

By Lieutenant Colonel Richard Tokarz, U.S.A.F.
Retired

The prospect that we may have abandoned captured Americans to an unknown fate in our haste to extricate ourselves from an unpopular Asian war will haunt this generation into the next century. In May of 1969 over Laos I heard a downed Navy pilot describe his own capture on his survival radio. His last words were, "I don't think they're going to kill me... I'm a P.O.W." I have long since forgotten his name, but I do remember he was not among those expatriated in 1973. The following story is based on fact, although the conclusion is pure conjecture. The ultimate fate of many military men listed as "Missing in Action" (MIA) may be known only to God.

Duan Li heard the low flying airplane as he plodded behind his water buffalo in the hot morning sun. The southwest monsoon had come early and the fields were wet enough to begin planting. It had been a kind year, this one of the Horse. His pigs had fattened well, he had sixty monkeys caged and the gold makers had made dozens of bracelets and charms that would bring many goods in exchange at the market in Nam Suea. The village women would be pleased with the bright cloth, sandals, iron pots and spices they would get.

Li would see Pere Culbase at the mission and deliver two large baskets of plump ripe poppies to him. Pere would be pleased with his "petites pommes dejoie" and might even trade a donkey for them. Pere was big and fat and had a bushy black beard that he trimmed with a special knife called a "rasoir", a blade so sharp it could cut without pain. Pere had several of these and gave Li one with a smooth ivory handle on his last visit.

Duan Li had received many blessings from Buddha. At age thirty he was headman of his people and had three lovely wives. He was an expert hunter and an accomplished farmer. His valley had known peace since his birth, but the Ammans from the east were stirring and there was fighting in the mountains between them and the Meo, a bandit tribe who lived in the highlands and practiced slash and burn farming, moving each year to a new place.

Li loosened his grip on the thongs that controlled the large bull. They had come to the end of the field near the dike and he was hungry. He leaped off the broad plank that held down the six evenly spaced bamboo spikes which gouged out the harrows in the muddy earth. Two women followed behind him, carefully placing rice shoots in the furrows and tamping them down. Duan sat on the earthen berms and took a leather pouch from his shoulder. Inside there were balls of rice and strips of dried monkey meat. As he ate he watched conical hats moving slowly toward him, bobbing rhythmically in the poetic cadence of a timeless Asian ritual.

The drone of the airplane was now loud and annoying. In the village children looked up from their games and people leaned out doorways, shielding their eyes from the sun as they peered skyward. There was a deep rumbling growl from the south that grew rapidly louder. The children cupped their hands over their ears and ran inside. Suddenly two large airplanes burst into view over the ridgeline and the small airplane dropped something that streamed a long trail of white smoke. It hit between the two large bamboo storehouses near the north end of the village and the two big planes went straight for it. Oblong objects fell from beneath their wings and tumbled end-over-end before striking the ground and erupting in a sheet of flame. Then explosions boomed among the flimsy houses in the village. His people streamed from their homes in panic, seeking to escape the hell that was suddenly in their midst. Fountains of dirt stitched a trail along the dike and Di-Di, the waterbuck, reared and screamed in agony. Duan ran toward him, then there was a deafening explosion and he was floating lazily through a dark space with moist clumps of earth.

Duan Li awakened to the wails and moans of his people mingled with the crackling of burning bamboo. He felt a sticky wetness on the back of his neck and thought he was wounded. He slid his hand slowly behind his head and grasped something clammy. He rolled onto his back and held up a severed arm with a gold bracelet still on the wrist. He recognized it and rolled back on his stomach, retching and sobbing into the rich loamy soil.

Two hundred miles to the south at an airbase in central Thailand Colonel Daniel P. Lee was pacing the floor in the wing command post. His outfit, the 414th, had just received an unusual task order. He didn't like it, but his three squadrons of F105Ds (fondly known as "thuds") were uniquely suited for the mission. They were to install a large multiple munitions dispenser on the center station of each aircraft in place of iron bombs. The big "garbage cans", as the pilots called them held forty bomblets that would be ejected in sequence through two ports in the rear of the dispenser. Half the fifty-pound bomblets were supposed to penetrate the concrete surface of an airfield, explode, and scatter shards of rock and cement all over. The other half were time delay surface explosives set to detonate at varying intervals to complicate the enemy's cleanup task.

The target run would be dicey. The drop altitude could be no higher than two hundred feet with four aircraft line abreast to ensure proper dispersal and target saturation. It could be a wild ride if the enemy defenses were up and ready. The surprise raid was intended to suppress the MIGs prior to commencing sustained bombing over North Vietnam. Why couldn't they just let the MIGs come up? Hell, it was going to be a short war with hardly enough enemy aircraft to go around. With all the experience his jocks had some were bound to become aces. Dan had bagged three MIGs in Korea and two more would make him a member of the elite group every fighter pilot shoots for from day one.

Duan Li walked unsteadily down the dike toward his smoldering village. He and Swan Do had picked up the remains of the delicate Loa Pi, his first wife, and put her mangled, armless body in the shade. He had to cut Di-Di's throat with a swift blow from his machete. The poor buck's entrails were hanging out of his stomach and red froth was spewing from his nostrils. Li choked back a sob as Di-Di sank to his knees, his eyes rolling wildly. He had felt the warm powerful back under his thighs since he'd been a boy of twelve and now they would work no more together.

Tears streamed down Li's face as he stumbled through the ruins of his village. The still and blackened forms were beyond help, but the cries from the injured were the worst. Why had this happened? Who among them had offended Buddha to the extent that his devastation was justified? Duan and the able-bodied men remaining built funeral pyres and gathered the dead. They would have to ignore the three days of praying that was customary prior to the cremation ceremony.

The villagers gathered what belongings they could carry and began the trek up the valley to the mountains of the cave bears. As they crossed the narrow river to the west Duan Li counted only forty-five Hmung, descendants of the most enlightened of the twelve tribes of Laos. There were just six children.

It was a slow and difficult march because some of the injured had to be borne on makeshift stretchers. At noon on the second day they arrived at the hunting cave that was known only to Duan and four other men. It was a large opening at the base of a limestone karst, which was protected by an overhanging ledge thick with jungle vegetation. It could not be seen from the air and a clear mountain stream ran by the mouth of the cave. It would be the ideal place for the Hmung to wait out the southwest monsoon and recuperate while Duan Li decided their next move.

"Kiss a fat man's fanny, Hadley! Ban-Nok-Nuk bombed? How? Why? Those people are friendly peaceful farmers and natural capitalist. Answers, Hadley—answers!"

"Mr. Ambassador, I…"

"You trusted Williams to mind the store while I was in Bangkok. Is that what you were going to say? If you want a future in the diplomatic corps keep those military types on a short leash. Did that… that… nincompoop give the upcountry guys the green light? Where the hell is Williams anyway?"

"Sir, he's downtown."

"Yes, Hadley—and I know what he's doing. Get his kit together and have him out of Vientiane on the next plane. If he's here after sundown you can start packing your own things-understand?"

"Yes, Mr. Ambassador."

Hal Fielding was in a delicate position. The North Vietnamese were launching battalion size probes into northern Laos and his job was to blunt the attacks with indigenous guerrillas and American aircraft flown by "civilian" volunteers while denying any U.S. military involvement. Last week's attack on what the operations people called a "Pathet Lao stage area" had been a setup by a mole in the giant command center in Saigon. There a slick-fingered Teletype operator on Hanoi's payroll periodically fed them bogus targets in friendly areas. It was Major Williams' job to correlate all target data with other intelligence sources, and he had been instructed to contact either Hadley or Fielding if there was the slightest question. Williams was a lush who had to sort out his world through an alcoholic haze. Fielding needed first class people in Laos to get his increasingly difficult and thankless job done and the Air Force was dumping its eight-balls on him. The only ones he could rely on were the young Lieutenants and Captains in muftis who were flying as forward air controllers out of Pha Nokh. Hal Fielding poured himself a second glass of scotch. He would need lots of it, plus a swami's cloak and magic wand to get through this posting.

Colonel Dan Lee and Broker flight had cycled through an in-flight refueling and topped off their tanks. He was leading the Air Fore's first large scale raid up north and had chosen the toughest target… Nong Binh airfield on the outskirts of Hanoi. The weather in the area called for scattered clouds at six thousand feet and ten miles visibility. Good for the attackers—and the defenders! They had chosen as initial point (IP) a prominent bend in the river ten miles north of the MIG base. This would give the impression that Nong Binh was being by-passed in favor of the hydroelectric dams north of the city… hopefully!

Dan Lee marveled at the rugged beauty of the terrain. It was desolate and foreboding, punctuated by sharply rising ridges of limestone karst. A plume of water spewed forth from a chasm below and spilled into a lush valley, forming a river that ran to the northwest. There were patches of white sandy beach and backwaters with aquamarine pools where elephants were bathing. The mist from the cascading waterfall formed an arching rainbow in the mid-day sun. Laos was a hauntingly beautiful land when viewed from twenty thousand feet in an air-conditioned cockpit. In five minutes they had crossed the Annamite Mountains into North Vietnam…

"Broker, let's clean 'em an' green 'em."

"Roger… Two… Three… Four."

The flight of Thuds dropped their external fuel tanks and armed the bomb release panels. The loop in the river that looked like a catcher's mitt was ahead and slightly to the right. Dan's navigation had been good. Their radar warning scopes started to come alive, indicating that the enemy missile sites had picked them up. It was time for them to slice down out of the missile envelope.

"Broker, go line abreast."

"Two… Three… Four." The wingmen drew abeam their leader and spread out until there were five hundred feet between them.

"Standby for the break. Ready… ready…NOW!"

Dan plugged the afterburner of the big J-75 engine, rolled inverted, and pulled it straight through, his wingmen in position. They went screaming over the river at five hundred knots dead on course for Nong Binh.

Dan saw the first spray of orange tracer coming up before he reached the airfield boundary. A web of red, and yellow dots joined it immediately. They were shooting everything they had straight up and the pilots had no choice but to grit their teeth and press on … Dan hit his pickle button at the airfield perimeter and the weapons interval meter began its countdown. There was a bright flash on his right. "Three's gone, lead." Dan said nothing. He was sweating out the end of the run trying to ignore the intense ground fire. Suddenly they were out of it, and the three Thuds turned south down the valley, hugging the terrain to evade the missiles defending the airfield. Dan passed a high bluff on his right that jutted down into the alley. He turned Broker flight west behind it to mask them from the enemy gunners and took them up steeply to twenty-four thousand feet when they were out of range.

"Anybody see a chute?"

"I saw his canopy come off, lead."

"Roger." They knew that ejecting at that speed on the deck was a virtual death sentence. However, nobody could say with certainty that Vinny went in with the plane, so he would be classified MIA. Damned shame…Vince Pellegrini was a great guy and a devoted family man.

Dan's Thud seemed a little sloppy, as he turned left to take up a southerly heading. His hydraulic pressure was low, too… "How 'bout lookin' me over, Two"

"Roger. You clear, Four?"

"Rog."

Nick Perakis slid underneath and slightly behind his leader. He saw a stream of red fluid trailing back from beneath the cockpit area and spraying off the tailpipe. "Lead, you're trailin' hydraulic fluid."

"Roger, How bad is it?"

"Steady and streakin' your fuselage on both sides of center station. There may be some comin' out the back, too, through the engine bay." Bad news. The red fluid was the life-blood of his flight controls. Lose it—lose the airplane. The pressure was slowly dropping and he felt an unscheduled pitch transient.

"Nick, get clear… she's startin' t' porpoise on me."

The nose pitched up abruptly and Dan shoved forward on the stick with both hands. Nothing. In seconds he was in a near vertical climb with no control and no airspeed.

"Hail Mary, full of Grace…" Whoosh—Blam—Whoosh went the sequence, just like they told him in egress training. It was a clean ejection with no flailing in the slipstream and no injuries. As Dan kicked himself away from his seat he saw he was falling toward a solid under cast below… "Good chute, Broker Four—he's got a good chute!"

"Roger, Two… Roger! I see it! I see it!"

"Let's circle above 'im. Get a range 'n bearin' off a channel ninety-three for rescue."

"Rog… I show him enterin' the cloud deck at one-six-five slash two-eight from channel niner-t'ree."

"OK. Let's orbit 'til we can get 'im on the radio. How's your fuel, four?"

"Skosh."

"Mine too. Broker Lead, Two here. How d'ya read?"

The opening shock of Dan's chute had been less than what he expected. He looked up and was reassured by the fully blossomed canopy and his bailout bottle was feeding him oxygen under pressure as he drifted lazily toward the cloud tops. His helmet was on and his visor was down. He had a complete survival vest with a spare radio and batteries, and was thinking rescue before he disappeared into the clouds.

Dan tucked his chin to his chest and crossed his arms over his eye-visor and oxygen mask. He pressed his knees and ankles together and braced for a plunge through the treetops. It was not long coming. He splattered through the top layers of broad leaves and crashed through the branches until his canopy snagged on something solid enough to stop his downward plunge. There was a jolt that felt like an upward tug on his risers and he was dangling in his harness, twirling slowly around like a lazy marionette. Quickly he disconnected his oxygen mask and took off his helmet. Then he unzipped a survival radio from its canvas pocket on his vest. He was heartened by the burst of static as he turned it on and began transmitting immediately. "Broker Two, you there...?"

"Roger, Dan, and the RESCAP boys already have a fix on your position. You OK?"

"Yeah. Good shape, but treed, over a steep cliff an' lookin' down a narrow valley."

"Any activity?"

"Can't really tell, though I doubt it. The valley floor is shrouded in a low hangin' mist. Only thing I hear is monkeys jabberin'."

"At least ya got company—no language barrier, either."

"And the head baboon just got your next promotion, wise ass."

"Roger that. And he's welcome t' fly y' wing on the next trip to Nong Binh. Dan, the RESCAP guys are up and should be here soon. We're BINGO fuel an' outta here, big guy..."

"Save me a cold one."

"You got it, boss!"

Dan turned off his radio to conserve the battery. He had another radio in his survival vest and two spare batteries in the pocket of his G-suit. There was a hundred-foot length of nylon cord folded up and tucked into his harness intended for use as a tree-lowering device. Dan looked down and judged himself to be about fifty feet in the air. The terrain below sloped away at a sharp angle and would be difficult to negotiate once he got on the ground. He felt the first drops of rain on his bare head and looked up at the thickening overcast.

The wind had shifted and was coming directly up the valley toward him. A gust of wind set him swaying and his parachute began slipping from the trees. He dropped helplessly for ten or fifteen feet until the canopy got tangled in some branches again.

It was one-thirty and the only sounds of life were birdcalls and monkey chatter. At forty-one, Dan was in excellent shape. His two-hundred-twenty pounds were distributed well over his six-foot three 'inch frame. He was uninjured, had all his survival gear and was thinking his predicament through. There was nothing he could do until the RESCAP folks came. Dan dreamed about Peggy and the girls and the loving support and understanding they had given him over the year. His oldest daughter, Pam, would be graduating from college next year and was engaged to be married. He and Peg would meet in Hawaii in July for a week's R&R, and he intended to make it a long overdue second honeymoon. Peg had gone home to Kansas and rented a house two blocks from her parents to wait out his combat tour. There was a good chance he'd make General from this command if his wing performed well. Dan couldn't fail as long as he flew his share of combat and took care of the troops. He dreaded the possibility of being desk-bound at the Pentagon, massaging staff papers in an office by day and egos on the cocktail circuit at night.

The drone of aircraft engines interrupted Dan's reverie. He couldn't see them but he knew they had to be A-lEs, old prop-driven aircraft with lots of endurance and wall-to-wall ordnance under their wings. He turned on his radio just in time to hear the aircraft transmit… "Broker Leader, this is Zippo One. Gimme some voice or gimme a beeper."

"Zippo, this is Broker—Go!"

"Ah, Roger. We're orbitin' your area above a solid overcast. Tops about fourteen thou'. Got a line o' thunderstorms boilin' up to the southwest an' headin' our way. Any activity?"

"Negative. And those cloud bases extend below the peaks. I'm lookin' down a narrow valley. Y' couldn't work here even if there were bad guys."

"Rog. Unnerstan' - we'll hang around and keep ya comp'ny 'til RESCAP gets here. Gotta earn our pay somehow … say, I think I hear Tim callin' me now on tactical. Back in a minute, Bro'…"

"Roger."

Major Barret "Bones" Skelton had a wary eye on the line of menacing cumulus building to the southwest. They were moving toward him and his orbiting wingman, and the radio was jumping with static as he heard RESCAP call.

"Zippo, RESCAP here. How d'ya read?"

"Yer slightly garbled, but OK. Go ahead…"

"Roger. We're forty south of the objective gettin' bounced around like a ten-dollar hooker on Saturday night. We're gonna hafta set down at Sam Phong 'til those bumpers blow through."

"OK, RESCAP. We'll remain on station an' advise the customer."

"Rog. RESCAP out."

"Bones" Skelton was not worried in the least about the nasty weather. The rugged A-lEs could take anything Mother Nature could dish out, but the extreme vertical gusts in a mature storm cell might set up a harmonic vibration in the big chopper's main rotor blades that would lead to structural failure. Now he had to tell Colonel Dan Lee that his pick-up had been put on hold.

Down below the rain was getting heavier and was accompanied by peals of thunder. The wind-driven rain splattered Dan's face with large stinging drops. His radio came alive once again. "Uh, Broker, Zippo Lead, over."

"Go, Zip."

"Roger. Seems our trolley is stuck across town for the moment. He can't get through the flooded streets, but we'll stay with ya 'til the cavalry comes."

Dan fought the rise of panic in his chest. He was drenched and getting nauseous from twirling and dancing at the end of his parachute risers. He rogered Zippo's last transmission a calmly as he could, then the storm struck with a savage fury. Dan felt as though he were in some bizarre Punch and Judy show being jerked around by a psychotic puppeteer. Suddenly there was a cracking sound overhead and he was falling! He could see the sloping terrain coming up fast, and then he hit in an open spot between two boulders and caromed down the steep incline... Jesus, Mary and Joseph, he couldn't stop! He sailed over a ledge and bounced on his back, the air rushing from his lungs ... "Hail, Mary, full of Grace"... he was plunging headfirst now ... "Oh Peggy, Peg"—the thought was shut off abruptly as his forehead struck a rock outcropping, then... nothing.

Two hunters brought the yellow-haired giant to the cave at dusk. They had been checking snares on game trails when they stumbled upon him lying unconscious by a stream. They picked up his silk bundle and used its long cords to lash him to a stout pole like a tiger.

Duan Li motioned them inside and had them place their inert prize by the cooking fire. Curious Hmung gathered around. The circle of onlookers parted as Duan Li strode into the firelight and knelt beside the silent one. Never had Li seen such a large man... nearly twice that of a Hmung! His, breathing was shallow but regular and a long gash spanned his swollen and discolored forehead. A murmur arose from his people as Duan Li touched the head of the sleeping giant with his hand. He had dared enter the temple where the spirit dwelled, and incense was tossed in the fire to appease Buddha.

"Will he wake up?" asked a young girl.

"Are his ropes tight?" queried a wide-eyed boy.

The thick patch of yellow hair tickled Duan Li's palm. Yellow-haired people were a sign of good luck. Hmung elders told of an army of light-skinned men on white elephants that saved their people from extinction at the hands of their enemies in ancient time. Surely the peaceful face of the sleeping stranger was not that of a child killer. There was an impish smile on his lips and his eyeballs roved playfully under his closed lids as though he were missing nothing in his dream-state. Li beckoned the hunters forward and they cut off his survival vest. Then they unzipped the pockets of his green coveralls, emptying them one by one. Women were busy dividing the orange and white panels of the silk parachute. They would have their new saris and bright sashes after all... Li bent over the inert form and studied his amulets closely. These no man could touch because they held the deeds of merit and of shame known only to Buddha, and Buddha alone would weigh them when the spirit left the body. Clearly this man was one of major achievement for he had TWO tablets of shiny metal (Dog tags) holding the records of his deeds.

Duan Li alone would decide the fate of the stranger. One so big and strong would serve the Hmung well. Li huddled with a small group of men on the fringe of the firelight, then beckoned to Sha Siao, the oldest and wisest woman in the tribe. He bent down and whispered in her ear. She nodded in understanding, then walked back toward the fire and ordered the children taken away. Then she began boiling water and crushing poppies, mixing the pulpy white substance with manai root to make a strong poultice. In another large kettle she boiled cloth, which would be needed later.

Li held the well-balanced rasoir in his hand. A flick of his wrist and its blade was ready, the firelight reflecting from its gleaming smoothness. He would do the unmaking cut that dulled the gleam in the eye of the beast and chilled the fever in the blood of men. He bent down over the helpless form as the faint uneven beat of helicopter blades was heard entering the valley.

ABOUT THE AUTHOR: See "Tiger Pause".

PAPA LIMA
By Roger Soiset

We all change with time; some for the better, some not. But typically the transition is a slow one, so incremental that we are unaware of the changes until we have reason to look back and make a comparison between past and present. On those occasions, the physical changes are the most obvious. Not so obvious are the changes in attitude, in disposition, and other internal mutations. A hunt is to be found in the eyes, the discernible changes that take place between innocence and hard experience.

Vietnam was an exception to this unwritten law of gradual growth and development. Boys whose bodies had only recently become accustomed to fitting into men's clothing were thrust into what Bismarck called "politics by other means." We were off on a great adventure, a war from which we vaguely knew that all would not return. It was serious business … but in such situations the mind often seeks comic relief. Some of what follows did not seem very humorous at the time, but the reflective person looks for the ridiculous absurdities in order, perhaps, to justify other absurdities… ones which were not so funny. Call it selective memory. What follows are those memories I choose to recall.

In June, 1968, I graduated from The Citadel and received my U.S. Army commission in my branch of choice, Infantry, Well, maybe it wasn't my "choice" - it was third out of the mandatory three branch preferences I had to list, and one of the three had to be a combat arm. But the Department of Military Science made a big deal out of it, since most of my classmates had not received assignment to any of their choices.

Pictures of the young Second Lieutenant Soiset before going to Vietnam reveal eyes showing pride, hope and trust. A year and a half later, after a scant eighteen months, those eyes had turned wary, fearful, angry and sad. An amazing transition … one that I shared with a multitude of my contemporaries.

The transition took place between late 1968 and August 1970, the transition of an eager, dangerously ignorant young man into a "platoon leader." The phonetic alphabet abbreviation for that position was, and presumably still is, "Papa Lima."

In late August, 1969, I arrived in Vietnam and was assigned to the 199th Light Infantry Brigade as a rifle platoon leader. My first few weeks, mercifully, did not involve any significant combat; one of our men had his leg broken when the shell casing from an artillery marking round hit him, and my platoon lost five men when their truck ran over a Viet Cong(VC) mine. Those men, it turned out, were on their way to "skinny-dip" with some young ladies from the local village while on a water point detail, so there was not an abundant sense of commiseration. All received a Purple Heart for injuries incurred while on their way to copulate in our battalion's drinking water.

During my fourth week while on a "search and destroy" mission, my company encountered a large North Vietnamese Army(NVA) force and as a result the next evening we did not set up our normal platoon-sized ambushes for the night. Instead, our company camped together in the middle of a trail intersection and each platoon was assigned a third of the perimeter.

I had taken the first shift on guard, preferring that so I could sleep uninterrupted until dawn. After the usual radio checks on the hour, I found my replacement in his hammock and led him to the machine gun position. It was pitch black, and I had to orient him to the placement of the gun and the location of the radio by silently placing his hand on each. I went over the radio call signs and how to respond to the radio check. He then indicated that his eyes had adjusted to the night darkness and was ready to assume guard duty. I crept away to find my hammock, which I knew was only some ten feet away.

I could not find it. I found trees, mud puddles (it was raining steadily), vines, thorns, rocks and even one of my other men in his hammock. Apologies were whispered for disturbing him and I continued my stealthy search. After perhaps two hours of searching I found myself back at the guard position. I was able to see the outline of the guard and another man, who I assumed was the next guard. Lunde, who I knew was scheduled to be guard at that time, had apparently awakened his replacement a little early in order to get the preliminaries over with by the time his shift had ended. I sat down in front of them. It had stopped raining at this point, but the darkness was total except for the luminescence of the jungle vegetation. I could see the outline of Lunde and the other man, and they both appeared to be staring straight at me. I decided to pretend I knew what I was doing, and after hopefully re-orienting myself, I arose and quietly crept off in the direction of my elusive hammock. Once again, it was not to be found.

I decided to do a search in quadrants, thinking that I had to be close. So I propped my rifle against a tree and tried to cover the area from twelve o'clock (the direction to the guard position) and three. No luck, and then I was unable to find my way back to the tree where my rifle was resting.

That did it. I resigned myself to being the laughing stock of the company the next morning, and curled up in the mud, Thoroughly exhausted, I fell asleep in minutes while the rain began again.

I awoke around four in the morning, and quickly saw that the moon had come out. I could see! And there, almost within reach, was my rifle and just beyond, my beautiful, inviting hammock. I said a quick prayer of thanks and slid in.

The next morning I was tired, but no dirtier than anyone else. I calmly proceeded to have a breakfast of C-ration coffee and a green can of something-or-other while the company slowly aroused. I was almost through with my meal when Lunde and the man who had been next on guard approached me with serious looks on their faces.

"Sir, I think you ought to know there was an enemy scout in here last night," Lunde told me. The other man nodded his agreement. "A little after midnight someone came up to the guard position and sat down right in front of us! I would've shot him, but was afraid I might hit some of our own guys." I assured Lunde that he had probably seen one of our own men who had answered a call of nature and was orienting himself from the guard position to find his way back to his hammock. He looked doubtful. "I don't know sir. He was mighty short - sure looked like a VC." Again the other man nodded emphatic agreement. They then left, feeling that they had done their duty. Since I am just a hair over 5'5", there was no doubt in my mind that they were talking about me. But I never let it out until I mentioned the incident in a book I wrote in 1993 about my year in Vietnam (The Two Dollar-Bill, published by Palmetto Bookworks).

Last fall, as I continued to try to locate members of my old platoon, Jim Lunde in Iowa answered one of my letters. I promptly sent a complimentary copy of my book, and asked for his comments. A few weeks later he called, laughing hysterically. He had never known the rest of this story, and told me that the only reason he had not shot me that night was because he was unable to find his M-16! Since he was manning the machine gun, he had no doubt laid it down, assuming any nocturnal visit by the enemy would have come down the logging road. As any infantryman knows, you are better off with a weapon that shoots bigger bullets, more of them, and faster. Wherever his M-16 was, it was not within reach. Thinking I was an enemy scout, or maybe even a dreaded "sapper," he had decided not to stand and try swinging the machine gun around before the enemy in front of him could fire. Another belated prayer of thanks went up after that telephone conversation.

November 1969 saw a significant increase in enemy movements, which in our case meant primarily small groups of recruits carrying supplies coming down the Ho Chi Minh Trail from "neutral" Cambodia. They were to join either the 33rd NVA regiment or the local mainforce VC battalion, the 324th. But the groups were not all small ones. After another day of our noisy cross-country struggle through the bush (our battalion commander was adamant that we move all day and ambush at night, with daytime movement all to be off the trails), we encamped in another company-sized ambush position. Signs of large groups of people moving down the trails seemed to dictate prudence. We were not alone in the bush. Around midnight I was awakened by the sound of trip flares going off - that, and the commotion of our men on guard moving and whispering urgently. I heard the sound of an M-60 bolt chambering a round. Then, bedlam.

The night calm was smashed by the explosive roar of two M-60 machine guns, and probably a half dozen M-16s at the same time. There were no individual shots that could be heard, rather it was just one long explosion, lasting perhaps three minutes. Then all who were on that side of the perimeter frantically engaged in reloading while our company commander called for artillery support.

After the artillery began arriving, the 105mm shells making a "whoosh" sound as they passed overhead to their destination, I noticed that the explosions seemed almost quiet due to the muffling effect of the jungle, but we could still feel slight jolts in the ground until the artillery rounds were "walked" further south in the probable direction of our enemy's flight. The company commander then proceeded to make a calm, and obviously proud, report of his successful ambush.

Meanwhile, the third platoon leader was nearly incoherent with fear, the action having been almost entirely on his third of the perimeter. His platoon sergeant, Tom Massie, took charge of a half-dozen men to inspect the kill zone of our ambush. They found seven fallen enemy soldiers, and prudently put a bullet into the head of each to be certain none were feigning death. The next morning, we found a live grenade in the hand of one of them.

The captain's radio conversation with the battalion commander was suddenly interrupted by another transmission. An "override" from another source was so strong that its volume enabled anyone within thirty feel of the PRC-25 radio to hear the voice of a Vietnamese.

"Yankees, you are surrounded! We are going to kill you all! You must surrender or die!'

Stunned silence followed. Then, the formerly cool and confident company commander started screaming on the radio at the battalion commander. The confident report of our CO had turned into a frantic demand for help.

"Goddam it, we need some fucking air support! And I don't mean in the morning, I mean right fucking now!"

He was assured that support would be forthcoming, and we all crawled inside our individual mental cocoons and waited. About fifteen minutes later the sound of an aircraft was heard, and again we could hear a radio conversation with someone our command post ("CP") called, "Puff the Magic Dragon," a C-130 aircraft equipped with miniguns.

Soon, a long red line of minigun fire was pouring down from a source in the night sky onto the jungle to our south. We learned that the plane had an infra-red sensing device and could aim accordingly. Six thousand rounds per minute, with a liberal percentage of tracer rounds thrown in to assist night aiming, created a nasty howl from the aircraft and an awesome fireworks display. It reminded me of a tornado: both came from the sky, and both had immense power, and in both cases, if a person was more than fifty feet away from their point of impact he would be untouched; but if one were much closer, he would probably die.

The company maintained a fifty percent alert for the remainder of the night (I personally doubt the half allowed to sleep actually did). The strange radio message turned out to be a hoax by some local HAM operator with VC sympathies. The next morning the jungle still stank of expended ammunition, and we all took turns inspecting the results.

Only four enemy dead remained. Their surviving friends had somehow managed to return and drag away three of their comrades from beneath the very noses of men already frightened to the point of hallucination. I was astounded that this had happened. We had all heard stories of how our enemy could see in total darkness and move in utter silence; this served to confirm them.

Long term results of our ambush: Sp4 James Solomon received a Silver Star, being credited with killing six of the enemy soldiers in front of his machine gun. He had never seen anything other than the flares going off, and never received any return fire; but he did his job, and quite likely saved the lives of some of his friends by doing so. Our company commander was abruptly relieved a few weeks later, presumably as soon as the battalion commander could find a replacement. Captains don't get away with cursing at colonels. And within a month, the third platoon leader called in his own medevac for "battle fatigue" in the middle of an exhausting but otherwise uneventful day. Those of us who were not laughing or cursing bid him good riddance.

By December of 1969 I had over three months of field duty under my belt, and thereby was almost in a "senior" position as a platoon leader in the battalion. At that time my brigade was still getting in enough replacements so that lieutenants could rotate out of the field after no more than five months. Seniority therefore played a part in assignments; the only ones who got out of the field early were those who had enormous "pull" upstairs, or who had screwed up in some way and were given a rear job as "punishment." Made sense, if only by Army logic.

The process of becoming accustomed to the demands of life in the field was referred to as, "getting your shit together." Appropriate expression, I suppose, since those who failed to do so often wound up with that substance splattered all over the jungle vegetation. And often, those errors were costly to more than just the platoon leaders. As a result, my overwhelming fear was of screwing up. Failing to react properly or quickly enough, not interpreting the signs of a possible ambush, incorrect artillery adjustment … there were so many ways to make fatal mistakes. And on top of all that, a prudent man still had to watch were he placed each step, to be certain the vine he was brushing aside was not a Bamboo Viper in disguise, and to obtain agreement from someone behind him that the bump on his neck was not a tick or leech that had buried itself in the skin and would require painful extraction by a burning cigarette.One of my last operations before finally being elevated to company executive officer, involved a search-and-destroy mission into an area of Binh Tuy Province. The report from Intelligence was that the area was "infested" with VC, and bunker complexes abounded. As usual, their report was for the most part wrong.

The company moved single-file into the area, after insertion by a flotilla of "Huey helicopters," with my platoon leading. All we could find after a day of searching was a single long-abandoned base camp. It had never harbored more than a platoon of men by our reckoning. But it did have one very unusual feature … a small mound with what appeared to be a trap door on its top. It looked like a miniature storm shelter. A few slats of wood were missing from the door.

"Sir, do you think it's a cache?" asked Sp4 David Mathis with eyes shining. Clearly he wanted to investigate. The second most popular dream of the grunts was to find a cache with SKS rifles, maybe even Makarov pistols, to take home as souvenirs.

I was more concerned with the nightmare of the grunts: finding a booby trap the hard way, and not having any chance to even the score against an enemy who had departed the premises long ago.

When Mathis asked if he could enter the mound, I refused and told him to throw in a "frag" (fragmentation grenade). His face registered deep disappointment. "But, sir…"

"Just do it!" I said in an uncompromising tone.

The rest of the platoon backed away and faced outward, to be ready in case the explosion triggered a response from any nearby enemy we had missed. Mathis threw in the frag.

The explosion was surprisingly loud, so obviously the "entrance" was not to a tunnel or even a deep depression. But the most noticeable thing was the violent emission of black and gray material, which flew up perhaps forty feet and tiny bits of it rained on myself and Mathis. We were the only ones who had not backed away far enough. "Smells funky, sir," Mathis said as he wrinkled his nose. After advising the company commander of the outcome, my platoon was told to stay in place while the rest of the company proceeded through. We would take up the "drag" position, enabling one of the other platoons to take the lead and be in position to make the next discovery. Every man in the company therefore had the opportunity to see (and smell) the daring accomplishment of first platoon. As they filed by, I tried very hard not to think of what was being said about the lieutenant who had ordered the demolition of an "enemy" latrine…

Shortly thereafter I met the man I had the utmost admiration for: my replacement as first platoon leader! I remember well my earnest questions when I had first arrived, my reluctance to show fear, and my dread of making a mistake that would cost one of my men his life. An awesome responsibility for a twenty-three year old, if he came out of ROTC - possibly younger if he had gone through O.C.S. The other source of commissioned junior officers in the U.S. Army was West Point. None of the above did anything to enhance the reputation of new platoon leaders. Despite training and personal effort, success or failure seemed to be largely a matter of on-the job-training and luck. Some new lieutenants did well as platoon leaders, others were mediocre, and still more were disasters. But they all had much to learn on arrival in Vietnam, and those who thought otherwise were often the least successful. I personally measured that success in terms of friendly casualties, although "kill ratios" were big with the commanders. To me, ten-to-one still meant we had lost a man.

My immediate replacement was unfortunately one who thought he already knew more than the men who had been in the field for up to ten months. He had gone through the Ranger and Airborne schools, and had acquired a disdain for "straight leg" infantry. He subsequently tried to incorporate some Ranger tactics, and two men in first platoon were killed. My initial receipt of the news of two casualties was followed within minutes by the arrival of Sp4 Lunde at the company rear area at the Brigade Main Base. He had flown in on the medevac helicopter, and then had hitched a ride from the hospital to the brigade base.

Lunde's eyes were red and ominous, he stunk and was filthy. He had his rucksack, but no rifle. He stood swaying in the door to the company building like a gaunt refugee, not saying a word. I quickly told him that I was about to run over to the 93rd field hospital where I was informed the men had been taken. He said that there was no point in doing so, both were dead; the new man who had been the ammunition bearer, and Lunde's close friend who had been the machine gunner.

The new lieutenant had sent the two out alone to flank an enemy force and place fire on them in order to drive them into an ambush by the rest of the platoon. It had backfired. Lunde had thrown down his rifle in frustration and anger when, defying orders, he climbed on the medevac helicopter to be with his dying friend. I was angry at the risky tactics, grief-stricken at the results, and most of all consumed with a feeling of guilt. I had left "my platoon" in the hands of an arrogant greenhorn in order to escape field duty at the first opportunity, and others had paid the price. My own eyes still carry that guilt. My platoon was placed in the hands of Sgt. Massie, the former platoon sergeant of third platoon, and all was well until our battalion artillery dumped several 105mm rounds on top of them. Massie was badly injured, another man was wounded, and two South Vietnamese Regional Force/Popular Force men(Ruf Puf,as they were called) participating in the joint mission were killed. The subsequent investigation was generally regarded as a whitewash of an artillery screwup.

Second Lieutenant Paul Ruchalski was the next platoon leader for my snakebit crew, and I recall how he looked so terribly fragile when he first arrived at Firebase Mace to assume his new position. Months later when we met again at a company "stand-down," I was amazed at his transformation into a steely-eyed, no-nonsense leader of a platoon of infantry. Bravo company continued with a ten-to-one ratio, but it was not due to any more casualties from first platoon. They only added more to the other column.

"Papa Lima" - platoon leader. The phrase still evokes pride and pain, sadness and fond memories. It was my personal "school of hard knocks," one that put all subsequent trails and tribulations into perspective. If I live another fifty years, I will never see better men in more adverse circumstances. And despite all the attention given by friends, neighbors, family and the media to current issues, I believe I will retain the ability to remain unimpressed at the comparative triviality of almost anything to the demands - and the costs - of war. I have seen what results from powerful politicians playing with fire they themselves will never have to handle; and so I have become a skeptic on matters of domestic politics and international diplomacy.

Yet I have also seen what "ordinary" men will do in the name of friendship, even without the support of their country. When caught in dangerous circumstances, good people do what they must when they realize that the consequences of not performing can be fatal. And despite faulty equipment, "no win" tactics, inadequate support, meaningless "objectives," physical misery and exhaustion beyond belief, our American soldiers in Vietnam did a damned good job.

As a permanently disabled veteran friend of mine (George Dorsey of Missouri) likes to remind people, "We were winning when I left." Despite physical limitations that would keep most people bedridden, this man put himself through law school on the GI Bill and is today a practicing attorney. While his statement may not be strictly true in regard to those who served late in the war, Vietnam vets are winners—those who served honorably, those who did not shirk their duty … and those who have maintained a can do attitude. Hard times can have positive results, but only those who have gone through it know.

You can see it in their eyes.

ABOUT THE AUTHOR: Roger Soiset served with "B" Company, 3rd Battalion, 7th Infantry Regiment, 199th Infantry Brigade from August 1969 to August 1970. He resides with his wife Nancy in Lilburn, Georgia.

A THANKSGIVING DAY MIRACLE

By Thomas E. Summerhauser

To this day I won't buy a goddamn Michelin tire. In the Big Red One's area of operation (AO) in 1968, there was an inverted ratio at work concerning one's health. The closer one got to Cambodia, the lesser one's chance of retaining one's health. When you got to the Michelin Rubber Plantation around An Loc, you were definitely getting too close to Cambodia. If you traveled a little further North up Thunder Road (Quan Loi Highway 13) to Loc Ninh, you were in very deep shit.

The French owners of the plantation were officially neutral, of course, but there was no doubt in anyone's mind that, either through extortion or outright collusion, their allegiance to the rebels was clear. You wouldn't be seeing any American flags stuck in those rubber trees. We learned, after the war, that there was an underground pipeline that terminated at Loc Ninh used by the North Vietnamese to funnel equipment in the war's final stages. We knew nothing of this in 1968, but it was no secret that Loc Ninh was bad news. Fact is our Division, the 1st Infantry, lost its Commanding General in the battle of Loc Ninh IV. "Clean Gene" Kantor one of our squad members used to say that if you just rode through Loc Ninh once, you got a Silver Star, two Purple Hearts and a star on your Combat Infantryman's Badge. I say rode through because we were a mechanized unit, transported by Armored Personnel Carrier also known as APC'S, "tracks" or "snakes". Each squad had its own track. Mine was #333. John Pooler, a guy in our sister squad rode in track #332 or "32" for short. We always took turns pulling "point" because "31" was the lieutenants track and was always second from point. The #34 track was always last. It carried the platoon sergeant and the 90mm recoilless rifle.

And who is John Pooler? This story is about him and its' been eating at my soul for twenty-seven years. I guess John showed up in about September. He was just another FNG (fuckin' new guy) and it was not a notable event. Because he was not assigned to my squad it meant even less. You see, in the war no matter how close you got to anyone, you never let yourself get so close that you couldn't do without him. The bottom line was, no matter who got "zapped" you were glad it was him not you. I guess what piqued my interest about John was that I heard he was an atheist. While I was no Saint Francis of Assisi, I was intellectually challenged by the revelation. How could anyone faced with the prospect of imminent death be without faith or hope in the hereafter?

Being mechanized infantry had its pluses and minuses. On the plus side was the firepower at hand. Nobody was ever going to wipe you out. You might get killed, but you were not going to get wiped out or overrun as a unit. Secondly, you got to ride rather than walk into the shit. When you made contact with the enemy you were fresh. You dismounted the track and fought on foot, carrying only your ammunition and water... no packs or rations. Your 'home' track was never far away. On the negative side there was a real dread of hitting mines and that happened all to often.

During the year I spent in Vietnam, I saw my base camp (Lai Khe) a total of seven times. At one point we spent three months in the jungle before returning to base camp. In October of 1968 we had a brief "stand down" at the base in Di An. I got drunk and watched a total eclipse of the moon from a bunker roof. All of "Charlie" Company got thrown out of the Enlisted Men's Club... again. Staff Sergeant Pena told me to shave and I had my only conversation with John Shelby Pooler. John had been drafted. He had a college degree and taught high school English. He was older than the rest of us, married... had a little kid, I believe he said, in answer to my big question, that he was not an atheist but an agnostic. It's not that he didn't believe in God, he simply saw no evidence of him.

Now clichés do not become what they are without some modicum of truth involved. There's no telling how many cowboy or war movies I saw that used the line about "never knowing whether you'll see the sun rise tomorrow" but in Nam that was the very, very bitter truth. It's how we counted days... three hundred and sixty five... and every fucking one of them was the biggest day of your life. Given that, understand how our hearts sank when the word became official, "We're going to Loc Ninh". I would never let myself think about anything in the future, not my R&R in Australia slated for Christmas or my return to the States in February. I could only think of surviving Loc Ninh if I was lucky enough and kept my shit together. I made my peace with God as best I could, took my place at the 50 caliber machine gun in the turret of my track and headed north up Thunder Road.

I should note that at this particular time we were placed under the Operational Control of the 1st Air Cavalry Division, which, to us at squad level, merely meant that there was a different asshole circling around overhead in a helicopter telling us to put on our helmets and flak jackets... but back to the story. John Pooler was always afraid he was going to die. In fact, I was told by Tom Firman, who had gone through training with him and who, at the time, was about three days away from being seriously wounded, that Pooler was preoccupied with the thought. Tom was the "thump gunner" in our squad who carried the M-79 grenade launcher; it made a thump sound when fired. He and Don Coughenower, who was about three days away from becoming the gunner on the 32 track, entered the service on the "buddy plan" out of Des Moines, IA. Pooler was from Wheaton, IL, a very nice suburb of Chicago. He told Greg Pauley, another squad member, that he had it made once he got home. Firman said that during training John was always a step behind. He was an English teacher, not a soldier... sort of uncoordinated... quiet, private and "not with the program". When they were all leaving for Nam, Tom was lying on his back in his bunk with his hands folded across his chest. Someone said, "Get up Firman, you look like you're dead".

And John Pooler quietly said, "That should be me". He became quieter still on the flight over and throughout the weeklong indoctrination training.

We were encamped outside the wire of the artillery fire support base at An Loc. It was "Charlie's" turf, where I had been wounded seven months before... the fucking Michelin Rubber Plantation. It was the day before Thanksgiving and the word came, "Rush north immediately and link up with the 11th Armored Cavalry". The battle of Loc Ninh V had begun.

By the time we arrived, the first day of the battle was over. Our snake was point for the company. We saw the whole parade. There was Colonel Patton, the son of General George S. Patton of World War II fame. He was standing proudly at the road junction of one of the entrances to the rubber plantation, watching elements of the 11th Armored Cavalry Regiment pass by. Piled high on the decks of their tracks were links and cartridges from expended .50 caliber bullets, a sign of very heavy use. As Patton beamed in glory, his men flashed us five and eight fingers... they had killed 58 North Vietnamese regulars (NVA). There was nothing left to do that evening except "circle the wagons" and eat crow for dinner. Some of us felt that the fight must be pretty much over.

Hal "Woody" Arnold, an aerial observer for Division Artillery, wrote twenty-five years later that he remembered a startling thing about this operation. It was one of the few times that he actually saw the enemy in large numbers on the ground. He made a low pass over the rubber trees and saw them running down a road toward the action. He thought to himself, "They're serious about this".

On Thanksgiving Day morning, chow was cut short by the "thumps" of many mortar tubes. Incoming! I was cleaning my .50 Cal machine gun and had even broken down the bolt into components when "Sieg" steered the #33 track into action. One of the minuscule springs from the bolt fell through the gunners hatch onto the ammunition boxes below. Well I found the damned spring and got the .50 Cal back together just in time to bring it to bear on the enemy. I did a lot of shit that day and so did lots of others. Our Regimental history, I suppose, will show that Charlie Company, 2nd Battalion, 2nd Regiment made four assaults against a battalion sized force of NVA and killed 72 without anyone getting killed in the Company, and in fact, became one of the very few company size units to receive the Valorous Unit Award for that action.

It sounds good, but a lot of guys got tore up. The 34 track took a direct hit by a rifle-propelled grenade (RPC), burned and blew to hell on the third assault. It was chaos. There were heroes. There were fuckups. Nerves were frayed and when turkey day dinner was flown in to us that night there were hundreds of stories to be told to anyone who would listen. That's when I heard it. That's when I heard about the miracle.

Like the Rogers and Hammerstein lyric some believe that "a hundred million miracles happen every day". I don't. I believe that when I was a new guy in Lai Khe, and a rocket landed one night right behind the latrine I was occupying, blowing me off the shiner without a scratch while leaving it looking like Swiss cheese, it was luck. I believe that when Jim Matthews took my place as second man from point because he felt sorry for me and got his guts blown out by an RPG five minutes later when we walked into an ambush, it was luck. I believe that when I fell into a "punji pit" and discovered that the only stake to find its mark was stuck in my pistol holster, it was luck. When the bullet fired by a sniper intending to turn me into a soprano deflected off a shovel carelessly thrown in front of me, it was luck. The #33 track was brand new when I arrived in country. One year latter when I went home it was the only track in the Company that was operational. I believe that when it hit a mine and blew up seven days after I left, it was luck.

I don't take miracles lightly and even when I heard about John Pooler I felt it was an incredible stroke of luck… "Did you hear about John Pooler?" According to Gene Kantor and Dick Fortich, it seems John was clearing a bunker overrun by the 32 track. He kicked off the cover of the bunker as Gene was getting more grenades from the #33. An NVA regular who was still alive in the bunker, opened up on John from as close as two feet away with an AK-47 on full automatic. The green tracers parted his hair, trimmed his beard, went over and under his ears, but all 30 rounds missed him. John staggered back and Firman moved in with a grenade to finish the gook. Fortich thought to himself, "This guy's going to live forever."

If the story ended there it would be only remarkable. When we were alone with our thoughts that night, we knew the battle wasn't over. It wasn't, it got worse. November 28th 1968 was the most intense day of my life. The NVA were stubborn. They were mortared, bombed by our Air Force, shelled by artillery and it ended the way it always has, with the infantry having to ferret out an entrenched enemy. The third platoon of "Charlie" company joined "Alpha" and assaulted on line after slugging it out, at close range, all day. The return fire we encountered can only be compared to sticking your face into the entrance of a beehive. The only way out for the bees is through you. I recall RPG's striking the trees on either side of me, while hearing bullets whiz by. I turned my head briefly to see what the other tracks on line were doing and saw a number of .50 Cal barrels in flames from over heated cooling oil. We fired furiously, desperately, literally digging up the earth with our heavy machine guns. Any little mound, any ant hill, any small hint of a rise could be the bunker sheltering the invisible NVA determined to kill you.

I haven't heard from John Pooler since the war, but he has heard from me. The Agnostic, courageous son-of-a-bitch died that day while performing a most Christian act. You can call it "noble" if you want. It's a free country. You see, Jesus Quinene Meno from Guam had received a horrible wound during the fray. Now any combat medic will tell you that the worst place to be during a gunfight is where the wounded lie, obviously because someone is shooting at that place. John didn't have to stop. His job was to call "medic" and keep going. But he stopped.

I found them there together. Meno died brutally, but at least it was quick and put him out of his suffering. What struck me… what really and profoundly struck John Riley and me too was that John Pooler, in his struggle to help tortured Meno, had apparently died instantly by one clean bullet through the heart. Of all the broken, brutalized, twisted casualties of war I have seen, only John Shelby Pooler looked as though he was asleep… like a baby in his mother's arms.

I had a lot of trouble understanding why the recipient of the Thanksgiving Day Miracle would perish this way. I wasn't alone with this emotion. I have always felt that God sort of set the world spinning and said, "Here, lets see what you can do with it." Leaving one's fate to one's own design. On a rare occasion he might step in and cause something to happen. I like to believe that on Thanksgiving

Day, God touched John Pooler who was a good man, but who had not found God and said, "It's last call, John."

I have tried and failed to locate John's family through the years. I felt they should know what happened to him. His son or daughter would be grown now. His wife remarried, no doubt. I hesitated to tell his story, but was given the blessing of other Loc Ninh V survivors. I must say, that if he wrote home that Thanksgiving Night, I'd be curious to know what he said in the letter.

You will find John Pooler's name on "The Wall" along with Menos', whom he tried to save, and the five men of "Alpha" Company who fell with them. On November 28, 1993 John Riley and his family accompanied mine to Church. When the Deacon asked the congregation to pray for the dead, at my request, he asked them to remember John Shelby Pooler and Jesus Q. Meno who had been killed in action in Vietnam twenty-five years before. My wife nudged me and pointed to two elderly Vietnamese men in the pew in front of us... brothers... who crossed themselves reverently.

ABOUT THE AUTHOR: Thomas (Tom) Summerhauser was a machine gunner in the 3rd Platoon, "C" Company, 2nd Battalion, 2nd Infantry Regiment, 1st Infantry Division from March 1968 to February 1969. He resides in St. Louis, Missouri with his wife Becky.

THE PRICE OF WAR
By Peter M. Loyd

When we first went into Vietnam in strength, we began trying to apply our somewhat imperfect knowledge of the precepts of Chairman Mao to our counter-guerilla program. One of these was, "Replace what you break." This was interpreted by the great minds in the five sided puzzle palace to mean that every battalion-sized unit would have a full-time civil affairs officer who among his other duties would process claims against the US Government, for damage caused by its forces.

These claims ranged from the tragic (Grandpa moved too slow, got caught in the crossfire) to the bizarre. The story I am about to relate was one of the latter. It took place in Pleiku Province, South of Dragon Mountain, on Highway 15 south, in Phu Nhon sub-sector. One dark and rainy night during the monsoon season, when Cyrano de Bergerac couldn't see the end of his nose, two of our tanks were securing a bridge from sapper attack. The two tank commanders were justifiably tense and apprehensive. The following radio conversation took place…

"Five-Six, this is Five-Five… do you hear something out there? …Over."

"This is Five-Six. Sounds like a whole Company of them. I'm going to shoot a little canister… over,"

"This is Five-Five. Roger, I'm going to do the same… out."

Throughout the night, the two tanks shot at the noises with 90mm canister ammunition from the main gun (think of a shotgun shell, 2 1/2 feet long and 3 1/2 inches wide), 40mm grenades and coaxial 7.62mm machine gun fire. The next morning, they found not a mound of dead North Vietnamese regulars, (NVA) but one very dead pack elephant!

Shortly thereafter, the alleged owner of the Elephant, a Jarai Montagnard named Rma Chu showed up. His wrath was biblical in its intensity, "GI, you killed my elephant!" he shouted, loud enough for all the spirits of the mountains to hear.

Our heroes replied, "We're sorry, we thought it was NVA out there in the dark. Can we do anything to make amends?" we asked using sign language and broken Vietnamese.

"Get tow cables and use tanks to tow elephant down to District Headquarters, so I can file claim." said the suddenly not so feral savage.

The tanks did as the aggrieved Montagnard suggested. When they got there about noon on Friday, they were told that the District Chief had gone to Pleiku for the weekend and No!, no one else had authority to handle the claim. The dead elephant carcass sat there the remainder of Friday and all day Saturday and Sunday. By Monday, as the District Chief was driving back from Pleiku in his USAID jeep, about 5 miles out he noticed the smell. At 4 miles, he became nauseous. At 3 miles, he commenced vomiting. By 1 1/2 mile, he had emptied his stomach and had the dry heaves. Semi-consciously, he drove into the compound and found the dead elephant on his doorstep, surrounded by several million ants with at least a Wing of vultures providing close air support. His fury matched his constituent's, Mr. Chu. He immediately got hold of the District Senior Adviser, an American Major and told him in no uncertain terms to get rid of Jumbo any way he could, so long as it was immediately! The Major, rasping agreement through his M7 protective mask, got an Engineer Construction Company which was widening the highway nearby to gouge a grave out with a Gradall, and the beast of burden was laid to rest in the bosom of the Central Highlands.

The regulations being what they were in those days, I recommended payment. Ultimately, the many cases like this caused the regulations to be changed; we stopped paying combat connected claims, no matter who killed the elephant. But Rma Chu got his blood money for "little baby blue eyes" and Chairman Mao and Chairman Ho got a good laugh at the dumb Americans trying to buy friends. In retrospect, it was another bright idea that was killed by reality... deader than an elephant!

ABOUT THE AUTHOR: Peter Loyd served with the 1st Battalion,69th Armored Regiment, 4th Infantry Division from January Through April 1968 and later with the 101st Airborne Division From December 1968 to December 1969. He lives in Louisville, Texas with his wife Phyllis.

ALMOST A MIRACLE
By Robert A. Hall

I wasn't feeling all that bad, considering where I was and why I was there. Of course I was hungry and the IV in my arm didn't help much… neither did the post-op throbbing. Still, it had been three days since the chopper pulled me out of Khe Sanh and two more since I came out of surgery. I was feeling a bit lonely as there was no one close to me that night in the Da Nang Military Hospital, so I was glad to see the Catholic Chaplain approaching. His eyes swept my blanket clad body from my pained smile to where the blanket dropped flat just below my knees. He sat down next to me.

"How are you feeling son?"

What does a tough, twenty year old Marine say? "Fine, Padre. I'll be back in the field with my outfit in two weeks!"

He passed over that bit of bravado to ask what unit I was with.

"I'm a Marine. I'm with headquarters, 26th Marines, up at Khe Sanh."

There followed the usual chit-chat: my name, where I was from, family and so on. We were discussing my younger brothers when, growing tired, I stretched out my legs from the lotus position I sometimes rest in.

The Chaplains face lit up. "Thank God," he cried, clasping his hands together and casting his eyes toward heaven. "I thought you'd lost both legs!"

"Come on Padre. How could I go to the field without my legs? I'm in here because they took my appendix out."

The sequel came several years later. I was safely home and a bachelor state senator, out with a young woman I'd been dating. She was gently rubbing my stomach. Suddenly she rubbed too low. "You've got a welt," she cried.

"Scar," I responded, trying to sound like James Cagney, the movie tough guy.

"My God, where did you get that?"

"Nam…"

Her face turned ashen and with a sad, comforting look she quietly asked. "What caused the wound?"

"Appendicitis."

She beat me severely with a pillow.

ABOUT THE AUTHOR: Robert A. Hall served as a radio relay team chief with the 26th Marines at Khe Sanh until his departure in September 1967. He later served five terms in the Massachusetts State Senate and resides with his wife Bonnie in Harrisburg, Pennsylvania.

ACKNOWLEDGEMENTS

Thank you, Ben Rogers for the inspiration to produce "Before the Memories Fade". It only took ten years since you first coaxed me, but it was worth it.

To Colonel Nick Sloan USAR (Ret) for his computer knowledge and help in formatting this book, along with Susan Sawyer and Suzanne Dana who helped with the editing, my warmest thanks.

To my wife, Patti for her encouragement over the years and to all of the contributing authors for their patience, I am forever grateful.

EDITOR'S NOTE: Above are the original acknowledgements as I found them written in long hand on a legal pad in Bob's files. The actual amount of time that it took to produce this book is closer to twenty years than ten, but who's really counting anyway?

Additionally, I know that Patti wanted to thank their families for the love and support that they consistently and unconditionally provided to she and Bob during his last few months: Nolan and Tiffany Michel, Michael and Maureen Michel, Sylvia and Tony Ruffel, Big Jim and Jimbo Caughorn, Debbie Billings, Kelly and Madison McCarthy. Patti also wanted to thank all of their friends who had encouraged and supported Bob throughout his illnesses and efforts to complete this book. There were those who called to say they care, those who came by to lend a shoulder or an ear, those who sent flowers and cards expressing their sympathy and support, and then there were those who just sent up prayers. He had so many friends, she and I didn't know where to begin the list, and so we thank them collectively. There are no adequate words to completely show our gratitude, please just know that we appreciate you from the depths of our hearts.

One last "Thank you," to Patti from me, for her graciousness and faith in allowing me to complete this project for Bob.

ABOUT THE AUTHOR - BOB MICHEL
By Patricia McCarthy-Michel

The birth of "Before the Memories Fade" was in the early 80's following Bob's 1976 retirement as a Lieutenant Colonel and his Army career of 24-years. Bob Michel entered my life in 1981 and we were very happily married in 1984.

Throughout Bob's successful civilian life, he never forgot the trials and tribulations that challenged him and fellow comrades during his Vietnam tour as a helicopter pilot. With the encouragement of his dear friend, Ben Rogers, he began to formulate the idea of producing a book that would reach out to others and allow their stories to be told. I will always remember him sharing some of his experiences, both humorous and serious, with friends and family. Their reactions were always tears, disbelief and laughter. The listener to these stories would soon realize that the war had greatly impacted Bob, but it was also refreshing to note that he was left with an unrelenting sense of patriotism and a deep feeling of camaraderie and respect for all the servants of war, particularly those he served with directly.

In 1994 Bob was diagnosed with cancer. The following several years were filled with surgeries, complications, radiation and chemotherapy at Walter Reed Medical Center in Washington, D.C. During this period, he began to think back to his survival of Vietnam, and that experience convinced him that he could also survive the cancer. As mental therapy during his treatments and recuperation, he worked and researched to give others the opportunity to "tell their story". Thus began the project of "Before the Memories Fade" and his eventual cancer remission.

Jobs, health, and other life obligations put the book on hold for a while and in 1999, but with Bob recovering, we decided to fulfill our dream of moving to Florida. We rented for a few years, continued working, and finally made the decision to build our dream house and settle permanently in Melbourne. In the meantime, the book material and correspondence had been packed and stored away until we would reach our final home destination. Unfortunately, while the new house was under construction, Bob received bad medical news. This time it was terminal lung cancer, and even through our devastation, Bob fought with all his strength to once again survive and complete his plans for the book.

With the help of Hospice, the last eight days of Bob's struggle were at home, where he yearned to be. During that last week, and among many heart-wrenching talks, he expressed some regret for not completing "Before the Memories Fade". Bob passed away peacefully at home with family members by his bedside on March 14, 2004. He received full military honors and is buried at Arlington National Cemetery.

I have since moved to the new house we had planned, and while in the process of unpacking, I discovered the box with Bob's book in it. Through the encouragement and hard work of our dear friend, Ben, we have brought life to Bob's dream. The years from the conception of Bob's idea to now have resulted in the stories found in this book, and they represent the memories and sacrifices of all the individual authors and characters. It is my hope that their work be enjoyed and related to by others for many years to come.

I loved Bob Michel from the bottom of my heart. We were best friends and soul mates, who gave each other strength, encouragement and respect. We were blessed with many friends, five children among us, and five grandchildren. The last grandchild was born just three months after Bob's death and has been respectfully named Robert William Michel. I am pleased to have fulfilled Bob's quest of over twenty years as a tribute to a man I deeply loved and respected, and I look forward to presenting our children and grandchildren with "Before the Memories Fade" as a glimpse of the man we all so loved and admired.

Printed in the United States
24771LVS00001B/325